I0014564

Stolen Security
Concern Intrusion Analysis
Network Management Hacker
Governance Responsibilities Violation
Detection Vulnerability Team Incident
Classification Risks Exposure
Confidential Defence
Impact Application Firewall Restricted Patching
Visibility Technology
Controls Requirements
Encryption Corporate

DataBreach
Cloud Password Solution
Principles
Architecture PCI
Username Credentials Attack Policy Login Loss
Threats

BREACH 20/20

Data Breach Prevention

Raza Sharif

Breach 20/20
Data Breach Prevention
Copyright © 2016 by Raza Sharif

ISBN: 978-1-5395-3751-9
Cover Design by: Cloud Swak

To my parents
— Raza Sharif

TABLE OF CONTENTS

Chapter Eight

ChapterNine

Chapter Ten

Chapter Eleven

Chapter Fourteen

Chapter fifteen

Chapter Sixteen

Acknowledgements

The breach 20/20 team would like to say a huge thank you to all those involved in the creation of this book. From the technical reviewers and editors to the readers, all of whom greatly contributed to this edition. Many thanks.

Introduction

Welcome to the Breach 20/20 series.

Breach 20/20 is deep dive security learning from world renowned security subject matter experts.

World class in their own respective fields, Breach 20/20 is a structured knowledge sharing approach to help you undertake an immediate security review and benefit.

This Breach 20/20 book covers Data Breach Prevention strategies. Unlike other material that you may have read, this book has been written to reflect actual findings, weaknesses and behaviour patterns that were uncovered during the breach post analysis phase i.e. once the breach occurred. In many cases forensics investigations and detailed research is undertaken to identify how the breach occurred with lessons that must be learned to avoid data breaches in the future.

We will examine at the key findings that many forensics investigators identified as problem areas and themes that were uncovered that appear to be consistent across clients.

As a consultant, I worked with multiple data breaches from the discovery phase to actual forensics analysis where I would search for malware to identify and catalogue indicators of compromises (IOCs) analysis. That experience and my own personal learning has been summarised to cover data breaches and the key findings across the data breaches I have worked on. The themes and the attack techniques that led to the data breaches and follow up recommendations/analysis is what this book is about. This book will move you up the learning curve rapidly so that you can see key areas that you must address which will help you to reduce your own susceptibility to data breaches.

I started security consulting in the very early days of the Internet taking shape in the early 90's. Setting up websites, FTP Servers and e-mail services for government services in the North East of England. I realised very quickly that the security consulting space would be a critical area for organisations and managers alike. Organisations would embrace the internet revolution, but without doubt would also need to embrace information security —what is now known as Cyber Security discipline. This would mandate that controls need to be in place to stop hackers from stealing their information, or disrupting their services via a denial of service attack. Whether the organisations hosted their own site or had it managed via a provider—it did not matter and still doesn't—security depending on the value of your information needs to be protected and viewed as an asset.

Over the last 25 years I have had the privilege of working in cyber security consulting with the particular specialism of data breach protection. I initially gained UK wide experience consulting in Government sectors, UK consulting organisations and then various Dot-Com boom or bust organisations or what we would now call start-ups based in London. During this time, I also enjoyed overseas travel to the Middle East—again security consulting. Eventually globetrotting across the entire middle east to include Dubai, Abu Dhabi and then eventually settling back in to tech sectors in Europe.

I am currently consulting in the UK with current engagements within various sectors as a lead security architect on a security consultant and advisory basis.

The motivation for this book is for me to simply instil the key security knowledge and awareness that is required to secure organisations. During my security consulting engagements over the last 25 years or so, the risks and threats have evolved. The security approach and methods to protect your data and prevent data breaches is the subject covered in this book.

A few clichés along the way will help colour in some areas of the book and to start with my favourite:

"Information Security has no end state – as long as information has value the threat will evolve"

This means that there is no panacea for security and no silver bullet. Securing your organisation is an on-going 24/7 process, which is made up of people, processes and technology. I would like to cover this very early in the book.

Those energetic security savvy tekkies that are looking for the latest gee-whizz tool for anti-hacking may be disappointed to learn that security is actually more about procedures (Probably 70%) and only thirty per cent technical controls. It's not finite although the last sentence is a useful reminder to consider when the technical teams get excited about the latest information security tech. Just to keep the record straight *I am* a deep techy, by my own admission. I have servers and NAS's and VPN, and FWs and Linux running. I play with the latest security tools and security testing open source tools. I love to spend time doing this when time allows. There are some fantastic tools and managed services out there; however, we must remember that *tools will <u>not</u> save us* but rather an understanding of what tools we need, and where they sit in the overall security model will.

One other point that I would like to make very early on is, that whilst this book covers, by and large, most of the key critical thinking that you should adopt, it is only just the tip of the ice-berg. My objective is that the book has both a light and appraisal based approach. That in a (relatively) short number of pages the reader can be provided with an end to end understanding of the key things they need to think about securing their organisation.

I have offered up advice and secured hundreds of organisations across the globe and in most sectors such as government, retail, finance, education, manufacturing, and law enforcement. I am now offering you the opportunity to acquaint yourself with the approaches used, the critical thinking required and the issues that need to be addressed in relation to data breaches. Whether your aim is to protect your organisation against a potential data breach or to merely improve your existing information security programme, this book has invaluable information that will help you through it.

As a caveat though – the advice in this book is my personal advice – yes it is based on sound practice, yes I have the correct qualifications, yes I have worked for multimillion dollar organisations as well as small to medium enterprises, but ultimately, _you_ are responsible for your information security not me. If you correctly practice the areas in this book, your information security will improve and your susceptibility to data breaches will be reduced.

The current evolving threat landscape

The second point is that there is no such thing as "Zero risk", it doesn't matter what you do, who you use, or how much you spend, there will always be an amount of risk left over. It is what we call *residual risk*. On a basic level, if someone really really really wants your data, with high motivation and the right creative juices, they WILL get it. It's as simple as that.

To really bring this point home, what we are talking about here is the level of sophistication that you may face from a state sponsored threat agent (someone targeting you). Should they decide to target you, they will have 100% success rate. However, the assumption is that you will not be a victim of a state sponsored attack.

This simply means that once we've understood this basic notion, we can then continue to implement the security advice in this book and deploy our security controls to protect our data.

Let me just repeat this **very** important statement: Your efforts to prevent a data breach do amount to *some* level of assurances — script kiddies and hackers playing with new tools and exploits will have limited success in compromising your organisation. You'll be able to address the low hanging fruit, **but** the simple fact remains, that the big guys, the advanced hackers (both individuals, the hacker syndicates, and the state sponsored ones) and their attack patterns in general, will have a 100% success rate, if the effort and MOM (that's Means, Opportunity and Motive) is there. In other words, if you have valuable data or sensitive data you will most probably experience a data breach regardless of what you do.

The objective is to adopt secure approaches to first of all, slow hackers down once they are inside your organisations with techniques discussed later in the book. It is also recommended that you encrypt or tokenise your data so that should it end up in the hands of hackers the data they illegally took from you is useless and obfuscated beyond any chance of recovery. You basically booby-trap the data within your environment, like quick sand within the temple of doom or by making one artefacts completely useless without the rest of the parts. This paragraph is **absolutely** fundamental to most of the book and is the essence of some of the well-practised approaches used in today's information and data protection strategies.

Common misconceptions

There are a series of common misconceptions that security consultants or practitioners frequently see within organisations. Misconceptions around having a secure, breach free environment. Misconceptions about being protected. These unmask themselves under the following guises:

- We have a Security Policy
- We spent 300,000 USD this Year on our Information Security
- Our Firewall won the Awards and is the best Firewall – and was suggested as such by Gartner and the likes (Gartner incidentally provide useful product information within IT across the board and that information is independent and is often relied on as an early view of a product set)
- Our firewall protects us
- No-one would hack us

By having such misconceptions, organisations struggle to understand why they have encountered a breach.

Well it did happen – and it happened because:
- You have a security approach but that approach is not integrated within your organisation
- You also failed to understand the clear threats and risks of your organisations
- You failed to understand the value of your data

Furthermore, breach protection is **not** achieved by spending.

Other possible reasons you experienced a breach are: -

- Your Security Budgets are not focused – buying the wrong protection
- Security spend – only a small amount spent on IDS –Must adopt balanced approach
- No Risk concept and inappropriate controls – No Procedures to support Technical Controls??
- No Monitoring to review control adequacy
- Audit findings are not reflected in Security Policy –Exposure / weakness stays the same. Security Policy is viewed as Product Selection – No homework, tekkies new toys

Information Security – A process not a technology

I just took a few minutes break and clicked the news Icon on my laptop. Top Stories: XXX site account holder's data exposed by hackers... the claim is made that vulnerable software was used to gain access to Passwords. An area we will discuss in later chapters in this book.

Raza Sharif

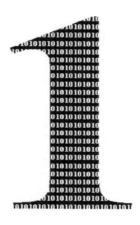

The Data Breach

It's 3 pm in the afternoon and as you sit at your desk, you notice a few senior managers running towards the CEO's office looking both anxious and serious. Glancing up at your monitor you see an e-mail from the head of IT that all payment systems and front end web servers have been shut down until further notice. You are both shocked and confused, how can this happen? The web servers take payment information for all your customers – something is not right you ask yourself. As your mind starts to race with sporadic thoughts, your manager, looking rather unnerved hastily walks over to your desk and requests your presence in an urgent full team meeting. All hands? What is going on? This must be huge? You questionably head towards the meeting room along with your other colleagues and the hushed murmured sounds of whispers.

There's a charged feeling in the room the tension is almost unbearable. As you glance across the faces your eyes land on a corporate looking man dressed in a suit, who you know to be the HR manager. What is he doing here? This must be very serious? Then the news drops. You are told that the card payment schemes have informed the organisation that some of their customers have had a high level of fraud on thousands of cards processed by you, and that it was highly likely you have experienced a data breach. You are also told by your manager under no circumstances are you to communicate with any third party whatsoever and if anyone asks you what has happened, you are to tell them that there is an IT problem and you have no more information. The stunned silence in the room is deafening.

(Actually the first few hours after a data breach are critical and what you do directly after the breach discovery generally indicates your level of preparedness on dealing with the data compromise and managing the communications to your customers, the regulators and in most cases the information commissioner's office. (ICO) is of utmost importance).

Your mind starts to think about what you have just been told — your data — your customers credit card numbers have been stolen. This is huge, your business relies on processing credit card details for various e-commerce sites in the online auction space. If you lose your ability to process this data, your company may close down, your stomach churns — will you still have a job next week?

Some of your colleagues are worried that some staff member will be blamed for this and others remember informing managers a few months ago that when you ran a scanner on your primary website last month - SQL Injection concerns were prolific; however, when it was discussed with the developer teams they said this would be resolved in the next live release. They also stated that the credit card numbers were behind firewalls so it was a "none" issue.

Your security team has been slowly ramping up and most of the team are mainly ex-IT guys with a desire to move into security. Senior management wanted an IT security department but wanted to get a few guys started from other departments before investing in training and there was also talk of hiring a certified professional such as a CISSP. You and your team are self-taught and have been tinkering with a few tools and even written a few policies for staff on USB stick usage after reading about the risks in the press. You had some support from senior management but it was always the case of we are investing as the organisation grows.

Sounds familiar? Read on.

This narrative is one scenario, where a small to medium enterprise (SME) will have limited security expertise. As a result, they will be unable to quantify and relate to threats and risks, and how those threats and risks impact upon their information or their client's information that they process, store or transport.

A parallel scenario is that large organisations have the investment, staff and the resources but have grown organically with distributed security functions in some cases across geographies. They also have a lot of point solutions to address security. They are a tool shop with little in the way of security strategy and integrated enterprise security tools. This type of organisation does not generally have mature information security policies, processes and procedures. They operate on the "security through obscurity model".

At the highest level and in the simplest terms — security models, strategies and defensive measures should be as simple as possible. They should not be complex or complicated.

Complicated security models allow malicious users to present attack tools and techniques and hide within the complexities of fragmented security approaches. We will expand on this concern later in the book.

So this is how your management feel. You feel bad that this happened; no doubt about that. How does your customer feel? You lost their confidential data and their card was used for fraudulent purposes. One thing is for sure, you cannot blame the customer for moving to a competitor. It gets worse, the internet is full of blogs and articles that your organisation has experienced a data breach. The latest development is that a staff member has found hundreds of your client's login details and their credit card numbers on public internet forums.

Day 1. You and your team have been told to be in very early tomorrow and the CEO is putting out a new message on the corporate website explaining that your organisation is investigating a data breach. You have also been told that the CEO has brought in a new forensics investigations company on-site who will be working with IT and will be on-site for at least two weeks. You heard on the grapevine the cost for this service is shockingly high and thousands of pounds per day. Their mandate, you have been informed is to find out where the breach occurred and to define a new security strategy to prevent data breaches occurring again, or at least reduce the risk of it happening again. This is frustrating – This is what you, your team and your manager have been repeating like a stuck record – day in day out the message that the security function needs to be improved as a matter of urgency.

The above is a 30,000-foot view of a typical data breach on the ground. I have kept this very light touch, in reality, a data breach is mostly an extreme event which causes considerable anxiety and stress for those involved in the remediation including senior management, business owners and the customer. Data breaches without doubt change your organisation and how you will deal with data security.

Data breaches also represent themselves to you and your organisation as a great learning experience. The goal however is to unlock this learning experience without having to experience a data breach (and not lose your customers confidence, your organisations reputational damage and financial loss).

How can we achieve the above? We can achieve the above by following the guidance and recommendations in this book and following the simple checklists which will provide you with a building block to improving your people, processes and technology focused around data breach prevention.

TAKE HOME

- Concentrate your efforts on detection instead of prevention.

  - Use the policies provided in this book to support technical tools.

- Security controls are actually 70% more administrative and only 30% technical.

Threats facing your organisations

We talk about threat in terms of, *the who* not *the what*. Threats have evolved and security consultants now understand that the level of attack sophistication has increased, but the level of knowledge to perform the attack has decreased. This means that a potentially devastating denial of service attack can be performed, in some cases, free of charge using online services known in the hacker underground as *stressers.*

To understand the threat question i.e. *What are threats?* We need to first answer the question *what is the value of the information we store, process and transport within our organisation?* If you are processing credit card information, then according to the US Secret Service, a single credit card number with a CVC is worth $3.00.

That means if you have millions of credit card transactions then to a hacker you have valuable information that they can sell. The value of your data will lure or entice hackers to attack your organisation and steal your credit card data for resale within the hacker underground community. A simple Google can confirm this (try googling "*Card Data dumps*"). Multiple parties can be seen to be selling compromised card data via various anonymous purchasing channels.

In fact, such solid credence is associated with some of the hacker teams and forums that once organisations get a hint that they may have been compromised they will actually purchase the hacked card data from the hackers to verify if the cards for **their** customers are included within the dumps.

If they are, they will then officially recognise the data breach and follow up by reporting it to the authorities, end customers, etc. **Let's just review that last statement**.

A bank customer hints that their card has been used maliciously and may have been compromised. The bank or payment provider searches the hacker forums to buy illegal hacked credit card data to review if their customers' cards are included in the dumps. Yes this is exactly what some organisations do, and accept that this game of cat and mouse with good guys chasing hackers is the accepted modus operandi of both parties. Some of the hacker teams now also have subscriptions services where they will provide you with regular information you can purchase illegally. We call this Fraud-As-A-Service (FaaS).

Incidentally, if you process card information, you will also be subject to the payment card industry data security standard- PCI DSS. We will talk about compliance and standards in later chapters but for now any organisation that is processing card data will experience a threat from data thieves/ hacker groups who will attempt to gain access to your information for resale and fraud. The techniques they will use will vary, from using your website for SQL injection to launching a phishing attack. Once inside the hacker's tools and techniques allow them to penetrate your organisation and network and subsequently sniff your network to collect and transfer the data, which is then sent out to the malicious third party server.

Threats generally target the C-I-A of information (a key concept of Confidentiality, Integrity and Availability).
- Information that has value must be kept underline confidential and have authorised users

- Information that has value must have <u>integrity</u>
- Information that has value must be <u>available</u> at the right time

Detailed threat catalogues exist where you can see the types of threats you should be aware of. A useful resource for this is the British Standards Institute – BSI Site. Look for threat Catalogue.

Threats and Exposure

For this high level assessment, it is not necessary to enumerate the threats, but rather it is sufficient to simply understand what is known by the organisation of its threat environment and how exposed the organisation is through its business activities.

The threats and exposure can be categorised as one of:

- No active threats identified and limited exposure;
- Threat state is unknown with multiple exposures; or
- Active threats are known with multiple exposures.

Visibility

The fact that threats exist does not mean that it will be focused on a particular organisation. Obviously, the greater the visibility/market reputation of a business, the greater the chance that its vulnerabilities will become known. This in turn will result in a greater temptation to expose those vulnerabilities.

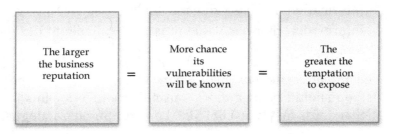

Breach20/20 fig. 1

As most threats are opportunistic in nature, it also follows that the greater the visibility of an organisation, the greater the motivation for malicious activity.

The visibility of an organisation can be categorised as one of:
- Very low profile with no active publicity of presence;
- Average profile with some publicity not specifically targeted at its presence; or
- Very high profile with active and focused publicity

Information Levels of Concern

It can be difficult and time-consuming to individually identify and value information assets; however, without an understanding of the value of information assets (covered later), it can be difficult to assess the appropriate degree of security required. For most organisations and its business activities, traditional concerns of keeping information confidential, while preserving the integrity and availability of corporate and client information apply. All of these concerns are affected by distribution of the information processing environment that is:

- The network environment consists of very few nodes, with limited distribution and no remote access;
- The network environment is distributed with limited nodes and limited remote access points;

- The network environment is highly distributed with multiple nodes, teleworking and multiple remote access points.

The Information Levels of Concern are divided into Confidentiality, Integrity and Availability requirements. The organisation's requirements for confidentiality can be categorised as one of:

- Majority public access information e.g. public web content;

- Significant element of privacy information e.g. internal personnel details and/or controlled information e.g. organisation proprietary information, processes and procedures, IP and Project Document;

- Significant element of sensitive Information e.g. CONFIDENTIAL or HIGHLY CONFIDENTIAL information

An organisation's requirements regarding integrity can be categorised as one of:

- A reasonable degree of accuracy is required;
- A high degree of accuracy is required; or
- Absolute accuracy is required.

An organisation's requirements in relation to information and system availability can be categorised as one of:
- A flexible tolerance of delay;

- The system/information must be readily available with minimal tolerance of delay; or

- The system/information must always be available upon request.

Consequences

An important factor in determining the overall threat profile of an organisation is to understand the consequences. Organisations should understand the consequences should one of the identified threats be realised. The consequences need to be considered in business or financial terms rather than in terms of the impact of the IT systems or infrastructure.

The potential consequences of an incident affecting the operations of the organisation can be categorised as one of:
- No cost impact or can be absorbed within the planned budget;
- Internal business functions are impacted, budgets are overrun and future business opportunities are lost;
- External and internal business functions are impacted and a direct revenue loss can be attributed.

Sensitivities

Another impact an incident can have on the organisation is to affect its perception. As a result of an incident, a loss of trust related to people both internal and external to the organisation, including partner organisations, can form. While it can be very difficult to place a direct monetary value on this type of impact, it must be assessed nonetheless.

The sensitivity of an organisation to an incident occurring in its operations can be categorised as one of:
- No organisational issues arise and it is accepted as a cost of doing business;
- Internal management impact and harm is caused to public perception;
- All levels of management are impacted, political issues may arise, and business relationships are affected.

It is important for you to have an understanding of the business sector that you or your organisation is in. Work with your colleagues and counterparts in Governance and Audit to create a basic register of threats your organisation faces. Align that list to your visibility in the market. This is a living document and should be updated regularly. Understanding your external and internal threats will help you in identifying the best data breach protection strategies. This is something we will dwell on in future chapters.

Threat Actors – state sponsored and MOM

Previously we spoke of the evolving threat landscape and threats from external and internal threat agents.

Threat actors can be broken down into three key areas which are:

- External Threat Actor
- Internal Threat Actor
- Partner or Third Party Threat Actor

The data breach prevention recommendations discussed in this book are constellated around external threat actors i.e. External Hacking which is still the most prolific in terms of attacks that target organisations. These attacks often arrive via E-Mail through Phishing attacks or simply from a downloaded backdoor and downloaded software tool or package. Sometimes the malware may arrive via a drive by download where the malicious file is injected within the browser that has unpatched vulnerabilities.

A significant number of major data breaches, over 50% (Source Gemalto data breach level index) occur via external threat agents and external hacking. That does not mean however we take our eye of the ball with other threat agents such as Partner networks that are effectively direct connections into your enterprise with free flow of both authorised and in some cases malicious traffic that is not being monitored. These so called trusted networks can be leveraged by attack tools and malicious users to help move your files around ready to be offloaded to a third party site but also used as an unguarded connection that generally have security controls that are more often than not rarely tested.

A very useful and hugely insightful yearly paper is the Verizon Data Breach Report. This report is a culmination of an annual review of hacker techniques across annual data breaches in the public domain and information on the threat actors, compromises and also a breakdown of the approaches used by hackers to gain access to systems to carry out a data breach. Please review this report now. It will help you with some of the terminology used in upcoming chapters as well as, specifically helping you get ahead of some of the current year's data breaches.

For a data breach to be successful three components generally exist they are: The means, the opportunity and the motive (MOM). This key concept is fundamental to your threat and risk landscape. If a hacker group has the means i.e. The skills (skills required are now not considered to be advanced. Attack sophistication has gone up but the knowledge to perform the attacks has gone down.) they have the opportunity (you never patched you Internet Servers) and the motive (you may have credit card data) then it is a fair bet that you are being targeted and it's not a case of IF it's a case of When.

Simple Intrusion Detection software on Linux sitting on the internet without any protection will be scanned by hackers approximately 9 times every 60 seconds. Some of these hackers are using automated tools such as Botnets that will automatically scan and attempt to compromise your servers and work stations. Other scans will be looking for vulnerable software or weak configurations for SSH or network protocols. If you're not proactive in addressing your security concerns, then your network or organisation will be in the cross hairs of the hacker teams.

In this new wave of Internet enabled devices and Internet of Things (IoT) we have become a digital connected world. We already have the humble beginnings of driverless cars, which are internet connected.
Is the Automobile Industry defining new security testing standards to cover Internet car security testing? What are the threats?

From a state's sponsor side, we have seen disturbing and alarming trends from foreign countries trying to sneak in to our world by using cyber-attacks, Trojans and malware, botnets to make in-roads to your networks that will perform keystroke logging. Regardless of the evolving threats and new technology the simple MOM model will help you identify any "Low-Hanging-Fruit" type concerns to reduce your attack surface areas i.e. Your potential for a data breach. A statement that you may find of interest that I can personally testify to, and that you can also find in the Verizon Data breach report is that "96% of data breaches were avoidable through simple controls."

As a checkpoint, it would be useful to familiarise ourselves with some of the wording that is often used to describe this whole threat and vulnerability space in technical manuals and also in general terms by security consultants as well as vendor product briefing on security related technologies.

Asset - Something that is valued by the organisation to accomplish its goals and objectives. A resource of value. May be tangible or intangible. Referred to as 'Object' Threat - Undesired act that potentially could occur and cause compromise or damage of an asset. Any potential danger to information or an information system. Examples of threats include unauthorised access, hardware failure, utility failure, loss of key personnel, human errors, neighbouring hazards, tampering, or disgruntled employees.

Threat-source or **Threat Agent** - Something/one that makes the threat materialise. Anything that has the potential to cause a threat. It is intent and method targeted at the intentional exploitation of a vulnerability. It is also a situation and method that may accidentally trigger a vulnerability.

Vulnerability - A flaw/weakness in system security procedures, design, implementation, or internal controls that could be exercised (accidentally triggered or intentionally exploited) and result in a security breach or a violation of the system's security policy.

Attack - An intentional action trying to cause harm. An attack is an effort by a threat agent to launch a threat by exploiting a vulnerability in an information system. It is the act of a malicious threat-source/agent; also known as Exploit (when taking advantage of vulnerabilities).

Probability - The chance that a potential vulnerability may be exercised within the construct of an associated threat environment. This is also referred to sometimes as 'Likelihood'.

Impact – Outcome of materialised threat Exposure - An opportunity for a threat to cause loss

Controls - Administrative, technical, or physical measures and actions taken to protect systems. They include countermeasures and safeguards. Controls are implemented to counter a vulnerability. Countermeasures are controls applied after the fact, reactive in nature and may be SD3 (Secure by Design,

Development and Default). E.g., Application Design (Design), Writing Secure Code (Development) or Deployment with the Least Privilege (Default). Safeguards are controls applied before the fact and are proactive in nature. Total Risk - Comprised of the factors of threats, vulnerabilities, and current value of the asset.

Residual Risk - The amount of risk remaining after countermeasures and safeguards are applied.

Ref: NIST Special Publication SP 800-30 – Risk Management Guide for IT Systems.

TAKE HOME

- Discuss threats with your team and document threat agents that may target your organisation. Who may want your data?

- Look at your business and decide how visible you are in the market.

- Identify your assets and consider how valuable your data would be if exposed to malicious parties i.e. hackers and competitors.

Risk Appetite

All Essential Security methodology recommends mapping between the risks within the organisation and the layered security control.

Risks must be managed and not necessarily avoided. There is a difference, and this can be illustrated by an understanding of the risk outcomes. A risk may be:

- Accepted
- Rejected
- Transferred

From a data breach perspective if we accept the risk we must ensure that the risk is mitigated by a particular mechanism. For example, with a denial of service attack, or employee data theft of your database—something must be done to mitigate.

If we reject the risk, we may reject it on the basis that it is an unlikely scenario. Therefore, it would be futile and not cost effective to introduce a control for an eventuality that is unlikely.

Risk may also be transferred (an example of this is to use a third party to manage our risk by way of a managed service or cloud hosting) this transference of risk may improve efficiencies by outsourcing but you cannot outsource your accountability—YOU OWN THE RISK. If there is a data breach, it is *your* data that is lost not the managed service providers or cloud service providers. This is a key issue to note. Risk can be outsourced but you cannot outsource accountability (generally).

So if we accept a risk as a real concern then the question remains how much risk are we willing to accept? A simple parallel may be that you have your car serviced and when picking up your vehicle the mechanic states he is just tightening the break pipes due to a leaky valve. What do you do? Say "No that's fine I'll bring it back another day as I'm running late?" or have it fixed? Of course you would have it fixed. So, you are managing the risk in your world with some feel for what is within acceptable boundaries of risk and what is not. This is the same thinking organisations do, albeit deeper and in a more methodical way. The amount of acceptable risk is called the risk appetite or risk threshold level.

The invisible line that runs through this threshold level is the comfort zone and where you may aim. The risk appetite level for your organisation is unique and should be discussed in detail so that you arrive at the model that works for you and your client and/or organisation.

So as a quick primer question: If your risk impact is very high and your probability is very high do we accept, reject or transfer this risk?

Risk Threshold

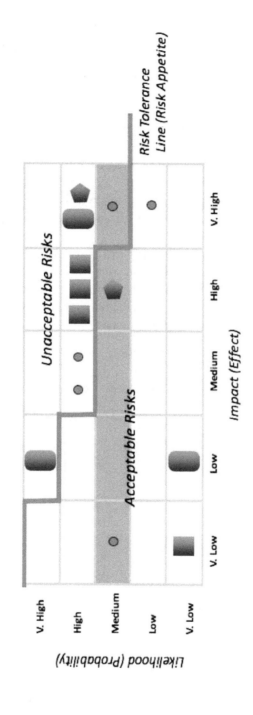

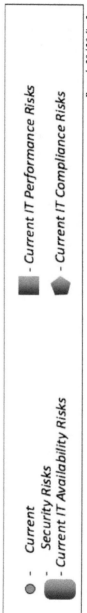

Breach 20/20 fig.2

Also because risk management is dynamic and continuous, you should monitor risks and dynamically address emerging threats before they become risks. As a security consultant, it is recommended to conduct periodic risk assessments, to ensure that no new vulnerabilities emerge as business and network environments change. Hopefully, you are not starting from scratch. Ideally, there will be teams or individual research teams, who proactively monitor the internet for signs of emerging risk. They are to provide guidance and actionable alerts in advance of new threats and vulnerabilities. Some activities within this phase are repeated periodically to ensure ongoing risk mitigation for an organisation's dynamic environment given the constantly evolving threat landscape.

We can say the risk of this asset being compromised is High, the likelihood of occurrence is Medium and the severity is High Internally with employee fraud, or an external threat agent. This thought process must be applied to all critical assets! RA should be performed to identify External and Internal threats.

Risk Models

Your organisation may have developed and made use of daily very well tested and sophisticated models to understand and predict risk, to understand the relative effectiveness of particular controls and mitigations. Some organisations have a dedicated risk department or Governance, Risk and Compliance (GRC) department, who can help you understand where your efforts should be prioritised in order to reach your goal of preventing a data breach. A simple risk model, as listed below, may be ranked by a Red, Amber or Green (RAG) status, common in risk reports, discussions and audit findings. At a minimum, the risk model should have:

- A clear description a breakdown of the risk in clear terms,
- The probability and impact of the risk being realised,
- A clear owner. Who or which department owns the risk?

The Synergistic Control Models

This model provides an excellent method to predict the relative value of any given control or mitigation in light of other controls. That is, it allows for the measurement of defence in depth. It answers the question: given limited resources, what is the next most important thing I should do to reduce risk in my organisation?

Asset Classification and Suspicion Classification Models

These allow for rapid and highly automated asset discovery and classification of technology resources. Suspicion classification quickly orders devices that are likely to have significant configuration, architecture, backdoor, connectivity or similar security problems, that are more fundamental than simple vulnerability testing.

An interesting note to bear in mind- organisations that have been breached are often requested by the ICO (information's commissioner's office), to prove that they have not been negligent in managing risk. This is done by showing risk assessments and risk appetite that have been carried out by the organisation. Proving that the breach was not due to negligence, in many cases, helps to reduce the monetary fines.

```
Cost of Protection Vs. Cost of Loss
```

A key question that will challenge you and your organisation often, is how much do we spend on protection?

During these times of increased efficiencies and demands being made to streamline and reduce overheads, a major issue that is often seen and that you may have seen or will see is that our line of work is a cost centre and not a profit centre as many other departments are. In simple terms it is not obvious what security teams bring to the table – the mind-set is that security guys buy new toys, restrict everything and whenever the organisation wants to try to evolve or introduce new technology – the security teams want more protection and more control.

It is fair to say that this mind set has not changed. We are a cost centre and we cost a lot of money but that cost must be offset against the cost of the loss. This is the crux of the matter. Moving on from this notion. We would not protect a simple static webserver advertising local community event with a next generation Firewall, IDS/IPS end point controls, quarterly security testing, red teaming etc. Well you may, but it would depend on the value of the information being hosted by both the organisation and the underground. The point here is simple and does not need to be over egged. The cost of protection must be based upon the cost of loss. If we have an understanding of the threats and the risks, we can build a proportional security model that is balanced and cost effective. Cost always matters – I forget the number of times I worked with security folks who would get upset at a PO being rejected for a new FW or WIFI penetration tool that hunts out Rogue Aps.

There is another dynamic here too – Security should be as simple as possible – a clear-layered approach will help you prevent a data breach, so try to avoid disparate and non-integrated security tools.

A lot of data breaches I was called in to investigate, had some of the most expensive tooling for data leakage and alerting. The problem was the tools were deployed without basic thinking of Cost of Protection Vs. Cost of Loss, as well as, no strategy aligned to cyber security kill chains. Discussed later.
In summary then:

How do we measure risk?

Well we can measure it by the impact on an organisation i.e.
The cost of a data breach. The breach will not just be $$$ value but
also your reputation. Reputation is also tangible in $$$$; in other
words if you lose customers you lose revenue.

Governance

I thought I would start this important area with regular themes
from a data breach investigation report that was experienced by a
large UK retailer.

Companies should conduct an information governance security
review, which may help them to classify their data so that they
know how to best handle sensitive data.

Governance is the underlying operational support and framework
for data protection and all aspects pretty much of information
security, technical or otherwise.
As part and parcel of your data breach protection, approaches such
as the understanding of threats and risks, you will also need to
develop governance approaches, which should be well
documented on what policies are available for technical controls,
what procedures are used for implementation and what are
acceptable approaches and what are not.

Governance deals with data breach pre and post aspects—thus before the data breach you should look to have a strong governance framework that deals with information security. Similarly, the governance team will most probably end up picking up the pieces after a data breach, and may be responsible for finding out:

- The causes of the breach,
- The effectiveness of the response to the breach,
- Any risks of the breach occurring again,
- What policies can be improved to prevent future breaches?
- Security Awareness Training

By examining the governance aspects of your organisation your ability to reduce the risk of a data breach will improve by establishing strong governance practices. In practical terms, this means that you should encourage regular design reviews with security designers involved in the early stages of solution development. You should insist on the use of test data for application development (only synthetic) and not live data, and you should ensure that security testing of code is carried out. The activities listed may be supported by policies but they will be implemented as a governance requirement.

TAKE HOME

- Perform a risk assessment of your security controls - measure your security effectiveness - aim for repeatable processes.

- Decide what level of risk your oganisation is prepared to take i.e. your risk threshold level.

- Define risk areas of outsourcing partners such as managed services and cloud service providers.

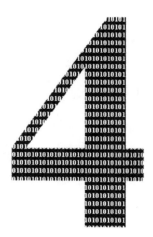

Measure your security

In a great number of organisations that have experienced a data breach, there is almost an egotistical view of information security. That view is that we have Firewalls, a full time security guy and a budget. We aren't perfect but we have the basics in place. This is a great start.

However, the fundamental question is, how good is your security? In many cases it is a difficult question to answer. Additional related questions are, is your information security aligned to industry best practice? Does it reflect the evolving threat landscape? The answers to these questions are critical, they will help you in your quest to reduce your attack surface areas and reduce your breach susceptibility. It is imperative for organisations, senior managers and security consultants to understand the effectiveness of the security controls and the overall security programme.

Information security is measured by its effectiveness. We can use metrics to gain a real understanding of this effectiveness. Security metrics are the tip of the ice-berg and a hugely interesting topic.

Security controls moving forward have a maturity value, which should be based on a capability maturity model or CMM. A security control may have the following stages:

- L1 Initial
- L2 Managed
- L3 Defined
- L4 Quantitatively managed
- L5 Optimising

Let's break this down for clarity. If you have basic processes your processes and controls will be at Level 1, they will generally be Ad hoc and Chaotic.

A level 3 process or security control, on the other hand, will be a repeatable process that is organised and documented. In practical terms one example may be a firewall change control procedure for opening up firewall ports. If any member of staff can call the IT service desk over the phone, request a firewall change on the perimeter firewall (with the admin making the changes without any validation or authorisation) then this would be an example of an L1 Process. Actually, this is an example of gross misconduct from the IT admin and the requesters' side. In essence the controls maturity will help you to work to a standard operating model for your controls. You may not be able to reach L5 processes and controls but the desire should be to aim for at least L3 processes.

Let's look at another example. The Dev team who are churning .net code for an App-Server with a Mobile Application that will connect from the Android Platform to an internal back-end server, have a security policy mandate to perform secure code testing or static code analysis (SAST) and dynamic code testing (DAST).

For a critical process such as the above, what level of maturity would you expect the security code testing to be operating at L1 Initial? I.e. The Devs do this when they feel like it? Or Level 3 – defined? Answers on a post-card please?

One other point to clear up is that we are now speaking about the maturity of the process and controls. The controls are made up of administrative and technical components in most cases as we discussed very early on in the book. So a Firewall or Data Leakage Prevention (DLP) are examples of technical controls but the methods used to deploy them, use them and what they report on are generally determined by the administrative control i.e. the policy or the procedure. This is where we seek maturity around the whole control, both the admin and the technical part, and where both areas work together synergistically to provide the control.

From experience we can also say that all the organisation's controls will be far from the optimised manage levels in L4 and L5. However, you should strive to have at least the critical controls to operate at maturity levels 2 and 3. An example of critical security controls would be:

- Network security change management
- Security testing – penetration testing
- Patch and vulnerability management
- Supplier assurance
- Security solution designs – i.e. Conformance to the organisations security standards

Please note the above list is not exhaustive and is an example of some areas that definitely require mature security controls. As part of the controls review, you or your organisation may want to perform an audit and report where the maturity of security controls is at in various parts of your organisation.

TAKE HOME

- Using standards such as ISO 27001 take a view of how effective your security controls are.

- By testing your security controls you will have a yard stick of your security effectiveness.

People, Processes and Technology

We started this book with the premise that breach prevention and information security is not just about the latest tools and products. We now know that data prevention is as much about sound administrative controls as it is about the technical controls or product. By expanding this type of thinking we can say that all projects are made up of People, Processes and Technologies.

In order to meet our security requirements and objectives we need to develop, if starting from scratch, a set of security policies. These policies represent a policy framework that covers all disciplines of security in all environments that affect your organisation. These policies are a complete framework and are related to each other and as such need to be considered in their entirety. This Information Security Operations Policy is a single overarching policy, in that operating procedures must be available and generally aligned policies to a standards based approach such as the ISO 27001 standard. There is sometimes a debate with organisations as to who is responsible for the creation, distribution and updating of information security policies. Without clear ownership of information security and policies there is a recognised blind spot. To support your data breach prevention strategy, you must have a clear owner of the information security function, which may just be one person. Either way he or she will be responsible for creating an information security policy and related procedures, which we will discuss soon.

Policy documents are high-level documents that set the mandatory requirements for Information Security Policies in line with your company's business objectives, legislative and regulatory requirements. For example, we discussed the credit card standard PCI-DSS—this is an example of a regulatory standard. Government departments have the HMG standards and information assurance guidance that government departments in the UK must comply with.

The Information Security Policy should ensure the minimum mandatory requirements that need to be met in order to maintain the minimum level of security of all system components in the organisations network and infrastructure. It applies to all components owned, maintained or managed by the organisation- including but not limited to all servers, hardware, desktops, laptops, patch management, audit trails, backups, etc. Furthermore, any third party that provides any support to such components must also comply with the policy.

As a general rule of thumb, Information Security Policy is the highest level and the technical procedures are the one closest to the technology. For example, a policy statement would be; The organisation will ensure that all external networks are protected by firewalls. A procedure statement may be that the firewalls must be placed between external and internal networks with segregated trust zones and trust boundaries.

There are hundreds of example of security policies from various places so a good start is the BSI ISO 27001 Auditors course, which can guide on the process of writing policies and processes, while helping you to create, deploy and measure your security policy effectiveness and establish governance.

Information Security Policy

Example of Security policies in relation to people, processes and technology.

ISO 27001 based:

- Organisation of Information Security
- Asset Management
- Human Resources Security
- Physical and Environmental Security
- Communications and Operations Management
- Access Control including Network Security- relates to Firewall and designs, Remote Access Policy
- Information protection policy – covers sharing protocols for the organisations and your partners
- Information Systems Acquisition, Development and Maintenance
- Information Security Incident Management
- Information sharing protocols, Agreements upstream and downstream
- Procurement Baselines

Security Blueprint

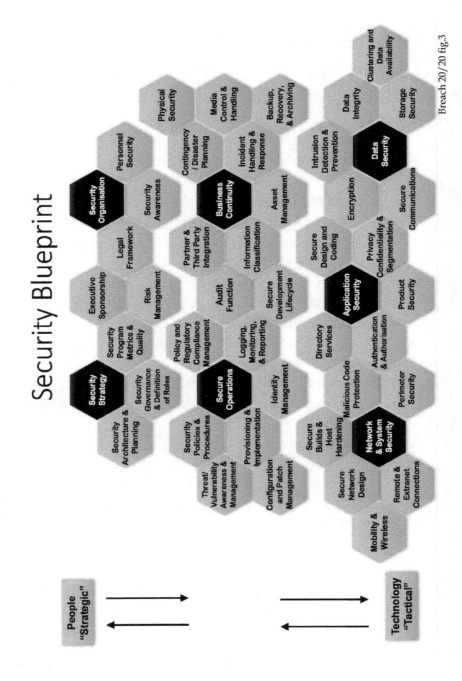

Breach 20/20 fig.3

The previous diagram brings together the essence of this chapter. Notice policies are higher up i.e. mandates from management and are also considered to be strategic. The technical processes are closer to the technology. In a security centric and medium to large organisation that has valuable data, the expectation would be to have all the above in place. Remember, if you do experience a data breach you WILL be asked about what you had in place by way of solid policies and what you did not and why.

Security Policy –Why?

Early in my career, I used to ask why do we need scores of policy documents that no one seems to read (they make the odd appearance at staff Inductions' or on the staff Internet and then disappear into the ether).

The reasons for adopting a formal policy on the security of electronic information are twofold:

- To provide a framework for best operational practice, so that the institution is able to minimise risk and respond effectively to any security incidents which may occur.
- To ensure that the institution complies with relevant legislation.

A central question is "what technologies are we trusting to enforce which information security policies?". Consider the following kinds of policy enforcement – controls may be technical and or administrative, physical, and organisational!

The Security Policy

Armed with the risk information we discussed in the earlier chapter, we should have a catalogue of risks and how they relate to our organisation. It's a living entity and must be done periodically. This is now called the Risk Register. Management should now have a stated policy on what their risk threshold level is and what is an acceptable level of risk. There is no such thing as zero risk. We have risks documented and we know the impact, likelihood and occurrence of external and internal risks. We can now ensure that our information security policy addresses those risks and helps mitigate the concerns.

Questions always get asked when people are told procedures are basically part of policies. Procedures are implementation details. A policy is a position statement about the goals to be achieved by procedures.

General terms are often used to describe security policies so that the policy does not get in the way of the implementation i.e. the doing or deploying piece. For example, if the policy specifies a single vendor's solution for multi factor authentication, it will limit the organisations ability to use an upgrade or new product. It may be that your policy documents might require the documentation of your implementation; however, these implementation notes should not be part of your policy.

TAKE HOME

- Your projects are not just driven by technology - ensure that staff have the correct training to do the job.

- Ensure that you have solid processes to support technology -i.e. your information security policy is the start.

- Define acceptable use policies for your staff and partners to ensure that everyone understands how you use technology in your organisation. e.g. Mobile phone usage, removable media policies etc.

Skilled Resources

The requirements to take forward the recommendations in this book depend on; the skills of individuals and having competent security consultants carry out the activities listed in this book. It is the organisations responsibility to provide the funding to help with the hiring and on-going maintenance of qualified security resources. They in turn, will strive by virtue of what they do, to help you reduce your breach susceptibly. Again, in most security centric and forward thinking organisations, security staff will be available and will be experienced. They will hopefully carry the various security qualifications and respected accolades such as the certified information security professions CISSP. This is the industry norm and your organisation should look to hire at least one person who is a CISSP and dedicated to information security.

Many organisations have a mix of IT staff such as network administrators and developer leads, being asked to take on information security responsibilities. Whilst this may work as a secondary or backup resource there is a fundamental problem to having the network admin (or similar), looking after your security functions. We have the separation of duty concern- where critical processes should be split between staff e.g. the database admin should not also be the IT admin and network admin. If this were to happen (and it often does) the concern is that this one individual has access to every system. We are not saying that we don't trust this staff member, but we are saying that this model is not conducive to security best practices used within the industry.

So push your organisation to acquire a dedicated security resource that should ideally report to the CEO or senior manager with executive support. The role would be a senior security consultant or lead consultant sometimes reporting into the chief security office. Information security has at its heart accountability and responsibility. The role for security consultants as well as the reporting chain should be clear, with a detailed job description. The reporting chain of security consultants furthermore should be positioned to avoid conflict of interest. Consider your security consultant reporting to the IT management? What problems may occur with this reporting hierarchy? There are multiple concerns with this; so let's look at one. You discover an urgent and critical patch that needs to be applied. The IT manager refuses it and overrides you because your reporting chain is in the same department.

It also goes without saying that you look after the security staff as you should all staff within the organisations. I really liked a cliché I heard a while ago "Train your staff to leave – and look after them so that they don't".

Information security resources or good cyber security resources are difficult to find. There is now the recognition that the industry now officially accepts the global demand for skilled cyber security resources and the problems this is causing. You will not be able to prevent your data breach and create and deploy strategies, without good all round security resources.

Aim for the CISSP and the CISA as good qualifications to get your team on board. Obviously the experience counts for a lot so look at the technical skills, and test them too with problem based scenarios during the interview stage.

TAKE HOME

- Look to hire experienced information security resources.

- Hire at least one certified security professional that carry industry qualifications such as the CISSP and/or the CISA.

- Encourage your security resources to attend regular training to learn about latest trends and defensive as well as offensive security.

Security Practice

I hope by now you are starting to see how security centric organisations and you yourself can look at this book to see how the foundations or building blocks of a data breach prevention approach are created. Obviously we have not looked at the technical aspects and security practice approach -which is what this section will cover. It is worth noting that security practice is much more than what we will cover in this section, but my objective when I sat down to write this book was to create a publication that is simple, clear to understand and covers the bare minimum to help you prevent data breaches. I have helped many types of clients, some of whom experienced data breaches, and others who asked me to help them reduce their breach potential or help them investigate the cause of a breach. I have also assisted law enforcement in some cases and various regulatory bodies, such as the Information Commissioner's Office and the 'breached' client. As a result of these experiences I have identified patterns of behaviour that were missing, and areas that were weak and would have gone a long way to reducing the possibility of a data breach. This section covers the core of those findings.

We will start with one of the greatest risk to a data compromise – Data Retention. As a best practice approach the organisation must minimise its data retention. It is recommended that the organisation limit the storage of sensitive information to a timeframe that is no longer than required to do business or meet regulatory requirements. If data must be stored for extended periods of time, it should not be stored on Internet visible systems, but rather offloaded to secure systems.

Furthermore, sensitive information that must be stored should be encrypted whenever possible as discussed. Data retention is normally addressed through your data retention policy and may be driven by regulatory bodies such as financial services. Either way you should have a clear stated policy on how long your organisation stores data in particular sensitive data. Do not just keep it for the sake of keeping it. The more sensitive data you have the larger the attack surface area.

Remove Databases - If you have databases or other servers storing sensitive information that are not mission critical they should be taken offline completely preventing any potentially vulnerable web applications or system vulnerability from being able to access the SQL data.

If you don't need it — remove it. A great number of organisations that experience a breach have servers that held sensitive data that were backed up in multiple places. Nobody actually knew where ALL the sensitive data was held. Apart from the Hackers.

Asset Management

Asset management, or a lack thereof, is another critical area that is a regular and persistent theme in data breaches. We should know and recognise that pretty much all device servers, workstations, and network infrastructure have an attack surface area. These attack areas can be targeted by a hacker to look for security holes and weaknesses. The attacker then uses those weaknesses as a pivot, as is the case in many breaches, to make in-roads to perform a full data breach. It is for this reason that we absolutely need to know what is sitting on the wire, in your network or your managed services providers, it does not matter; however, we need to know what assets we have and what they are connected too. Assets or any IT systems need to be patched and scanned for vulnerabilities.

We will discuss this later, but the start is to ensure we build a solid asset management approach. This includes a solid policy, technical procedure on how you do this and the§ outcome of a living accurate register that is close to real time of what is in your estate on-site, in your disaster recovery site, in your cloud service providers and managed service or hosted data centres. The premise is simple – If you don't know what's in your network, how do you know if it is secure or not? We are not just talking about your physical assets; we are also talking about your data repositories. Which enclaves contain your sensitive data? Where are the crown jewels?

OK, so you know where your crown jewels are (your database server sits in and has the following IP address), do you also know if any backups have been made on the SAN? Where the SAN sits? And if the SAN is backed up onto a NAS at your DR site? So, you don't have one set of crown jewels – you have multiple copies that all need to be identified by location and secured. You get the picture.

 Although we jumped into the database assets discussion right away (deliberately to show how important asset management is), the primary objective is to know where your IT assets are so that we can risk assess them, run tools on them to see how secure they are (vulnerability scanning) and rank them by risk.

On the many engagements I have worked on I have only found *a few* organisations with huge security and IT budgets that have got this asset management piece correct. It is *so* important. The others just sort of muddled through with spread sheets, occasional updates from finance and have IT teams sporadically running a few tools to see what responds to pings etc. then save the results in various excel spread sheets.

In many data breaches we find that the organisations had multiple copies of virtual servers running with a live backup of the database within their staging environment that were forgotten about and subsequently compromised. The security of those servers was weak because the organisations used them as test servers, and no one was prepared to spend time on securing them as they were "only used for testing".

So while we are on the subject of crown jewels and your valued data, let's try to answer an important question – How far do we go with asset identification?

Yes, we want to list our servers, desktops, firewalls etc. but what about media? Do we actually want to list every USB stick and DVD and CD in the organisation? Well, if you posed this question to an organisation that's actually lost DVD's and CD's containing very sensitive or personal identifiable information, I think you would find the answer an emphatic YES! YES, we definitely need to track and manage the asset information, and record the details with allocated serial numbers for all media containing your crown jewels – your data!

Key take home here is that data breaches don't just occur over the internet with sophisticated weaponised malware and payload infiltrating your internet's demilitarised zones. Some data breaches are simply due to loss of physical media, such as removable media or losing a Laptop that was not encrypted. These data breaches were not necessarily as a result of malicious threat actors; some breaches are actual accidental threats that we read about every day in the press.

Simple human error and mistakes can play a major contributing part to a breach. So don't always think technical attacks, think beyond this mind set. A favourite one of mine which I talk to my clients about is the print out picked up from the office printer with your print outs. You go to printer and pick up your print but also pick up someone elses, which is a network diagram which has IP address lists in excel.

The staff member takes his print outs home because they think it's just a few blank forms that they had printed and don't even shred the material (They didn't think they needed too as it was just a few non-confidential forms) They are forgotten about and end up in the trash or the street. Someone picks it up and uses the information for attack profiling and planning. How do you mitigate what appears to be a far-fetched scenario? What is that likelihood? What is the impact? Well for one, a data classification exercise would help - a topic discussed latter in the book which would state the level of confidentiality for all documents, whereby highly confidential documents would only be sent to a secure printer which is operated by a fob. Remember human error will always be present and we try wherever possible to mitigate against human error.

Another very good reason we need to manage our assets and asset identifications is that before vulnerabilities can be identified, the systems and network devices attached to the network – the assets – must be identified through a process called asset identification.

To be effective, asset identification must:

- Identify both static and mobile systems.

- Uniquely identify systems so that mobile devices can be tracked and systems with multiple interfaces are identified as a single system.

- Identify the type of asset, the operating system, and the services that are available on the asset.

Organisations may choose to perform asset identification by using an asset management tool and there are many and also outside the scope of this book. However, the information from the tool may be imported into the vulnerability management system to provide the list of systems to examine.

Lists provided by asset management systems should be augmented by some type of network scan, so that unmanaged or unauthorised assets can be discovered.

Network Asset discovery can be performed at a technical level through the use of any or all of the following techniques:

- Direct input from an asset management system or by the administrator.
- Network scans, including ping sweeps, Transmission Control Protocol (TCP) scans, and User Datagram Protocol (UDP) scans.
- Infrastructure examination, including an examination of DNS records, and switch or router Address Resolution Protocol (ARP) caches.
- Network traffic monitoring, including ARP and Dynamic Host Control Protocol (DHCP) requests and other broadcast traffic.

Do not use any of these techniques without formal approval from your security department and IT department. As in many cases the approaches can resemble an attack and your IDS/IPS and firewalls will be dealing with asset discovery as an attack, if not performed properly.

Each of the four techniques can provide a good list of assets, but each technique may also miss some assets. For example, routers or firewalls may block Internet Control Message Protocol (ICMP) echo requests or echo reply messages to some network segments, the DNS records may not be up-to-date, and the network segment with some systems may not be monitored; therefore, some ARP requests (which do not transit network segment boundaries) may be missed. The use of multiple techniques can greatly increase the system's ability to identify assets.

Assets can be categorised by their responses to scans. Certain ports may be open if a particular operating system is installed on an asset. For example, Microsoft Windows systems tend to have TCP port 139 open. Although finding a system with TCP port 139 open is not a definitive indication that a Windows system exists, it can be used as a starting point. Scanners may examine the banners provided by the systems. For example, an asset with TCP port 22 (SSH) open may show an operating system banner if the scanner connects to the port. The banner may provide some information, but that information may not be definitive because the system administrators can change banners. Tools such as Nmap also use operating system fingerprinting to identify an asset's operating system by how it responds to certain packets.

Static assets can be identified by their Internet Protocol (IP) addresses. This does not work for mobile assets (such as those that use DHCP addresses), or assets that have multiple network interfaces. Media access control (MAC) addresses can be used to uniquely identify a particular network interface. System names and NetBIOS names are used by some vulnerability management systems (in conjunction with MAC addresses) to track assets and to identify assets with multiple network interfaces.

Vulnerability management systems that use agents, also provide unique identifiers for those agents so that the vulnerability management system knows which asset is being addressed.

Server or desktop systems are not the only assets to identify. Network devices, such as routers and switches should also be identified as should any device that responds on an IP address (including printers). These devices may have vulnerabilities, or they may be assets that are unknown to the organisation. In either case, they must be identified if the vulnerability management system is to be comprehensive.

Typically, the decision about which assets are tracked and managed is based upon the value of the device. However, a network asset discovery will not satisfactorily address devices that are low cost, but contain business-critical data, such as memory sticks. This decision should be based solely upon the risk and exposure associated with lost data. Regulated industries (such as financial services, healthcare, insurance) and non-regulated industries and organisations with highly sensitive data (such as government agencies), have found that detailed tracking is a necessity.

One other key driver for your IT asset management approach, is to ensure you stay abreast of your software licensing challenges. How many staff are using licensed Microsoft Office or other software? Using software without a licence, as you are aware, is actually breaking the law.

Moving forward, we are also seeing more employees selecting their own computing formats for work-related functions. Installing discovery and inventory agents on devices not owned by the company creates security conflicts and leads to more challenges from an asset discovery perspective.

Global organisations need to be aware that there are local laws that can restrict close monitoring of devices. The cost and complexity greatly increase with each new device added to and require a clear understanding of the value proposition to determine whether an asset should be managed according to these six criteria is shown below:

- Cost
- Services
- Data security
- Shared use
- Location and unmanaged

There is another critical area that I would like to share with you, which is specialised data sets and data discovery. It is not uncommon for organisations to have flat files or databases without encryption containing sensitive data, credit card data, national insurance numbers, tax information and many other formats.

There are a number of tools that with a supported policy and procedure can assist greatly to help you perform a data discovery exercise. Regularly scanning your servers and estate for sensitive data so that it may be identified, catalogued and protected.

Some of the supported formats for these sorts of approaches include but are not limited to: -

Payment Card formats identified:

- All major schemes - American Express, Diners Club, Discover, JCB, MasterCard, Visa, and others
- All scheme issued types - Consumer, Premium, Corporate, Prepaid, Post-paid, Debit, Credit
- All known structures - 14,15,16,17-19-digit card lengths
- Specialist flags for prohibited data - Track1 / Track2
- ASCII/Clear Text
- Over 120 known PAN storage structures recognised

Mail Client and Server file support:

- MS Outlook formats (PST, DBX) 32/64 bit variants
- MS Exchange 2003, 2007, 2010
- MS SQL
- Oracle
- MBox (Thunderbird, Sendmail, Postfix, Exim, Eudora, and others)

Use of the tools is outside the scope of this book, but it is highly recommended that you use these tools which are both commercial and open source — freeware. By adopting these approaches, you may discover hidden data that would otherwise be obfuscated within databases and servers only to be found later and possibly compromised maliciously or accidentally.

The collected data is generally placed in a portal, application or a simple spread sheet. There should be a feed into the configuration management databases or CMDB. This is another area that lists configurations for your assets for build purposes. Again, mature organisations will have mature Level 2 plus processes in both asset identification and management, as well as a working CMDB.

TAKE HOME

- Create a list of your assets, building an inventory of systems, and data sets that contain your data or your customers' data.

- Concentrate your efforts on data breach detection and containment i.e. stopping malware moving around your network or enterprise. Data breach prevention is futile - expect to be breached!

- Look at your systems and how much you know about their security health – how would you know if a virus is detected?

- Implement protective and defensive approaches to protect your data.

- Design your systems around a defence in depth approach - i.e. multi layered security model. This means that you must have multiple failure before data can be leaked outside of your organisation.

Patch Management

Patch management and vulnerability scanning are closely linked and equally critical in helping you to reduce your data breach susceptibility.

IT systems have operating systems and firmware. Your internally developed custom applications also reside on operating systems. These systems will from time to time require updates, either from the Vendor or in case of customer applications as the result of product upgrade or feature improvement. From an information security perspective, the OS is a huge attack surface area that keeps security consultants awake at night. This is because hackers perform detailed research on how to bypass the OS security one way or another. The hackers spend copious amounts of time looking at bypassing techniques for authentication systems, a weakness in the way the OS stores data in the memory, or a technique to allow an attacker to elevate their privilege to gain administrator or root access. We call these weaknesses that have been found vulnerabilities.

Once they are discussed openly, the vendors will report this to the system users and release a patch. The quicker the patch is applied the better - the security consultant should be aware that if you have a vulnerable server on the internet or indeed internally that has a discovered weakness, it is only a matter of time until a hacker group creates a tool to exploit this vulnerability, which may contribute towards a data breach.

So first off it is essential for organisations to visit a list of bulletins, vendor sites and subscription services that communicate vulnerabilities. This area is called threat intelligence and cannot be understated. It is uber critical. You now have an IT asset management system so you know what OS your servers are running; therefore, if you find the latest windows server has a new patch for a vulnerability you must act fast. We are not just talking about operating systems either.

Think about the recent Heartbleed vulnerability or shell shock that impacted digital certificates services. It was critical, so to get a step ahead of the hackers you needed to patch. A large organisation with 10,000 servers across 8 geographies will be challenged to do this, but only by planning for such a scenario will you have insight in to how to deal with significant vulnerabilities. We mentioned vulnerabilities and the severity of a vulnerability, well the system we use to determine criticality is formally known as the common vulnerability scoring system or CVSS. This system provides a score in relation to the scoring of the severity of the vulnerability and how critical the vulnerability is. This is helpful to guide your efforts and help you understand how fast you are to react and deploy the patch.

We will come back to CVSS soon but for now please review the following chart:

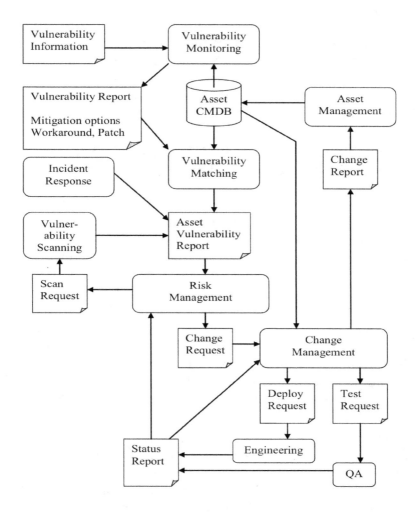

Breach 20/20 fig.4

The Patching Process

Patch management is of such criticality that a breakdown of the process and an actual template approach is given for you to follow as an interim. We also repeat this approach in the next chapter for vulnerability scanning and management, as it is an essential critical activity too.

If you do not have a patch management policy — stop what you are doing and start with this area now.

A great number of data breaches are constellated around lack of patch management and servers that had not been patched for a critical vulnerability. During forensics investigations tools created by the hacker team, which exploited that particular vulnerability, are often found. NB: In most forensics investigations hacker's remove traces of the tools and commands used, but they can be data carved to reveal a method that can further identify signatures proving use of a particular tool. We stated earlier that many breaches could have been avoided if basic controls were in-place. Well – this is one of those areas. Patch management is the single most critical and definite way of getting the attack surface down on your environment and reducing your breach susceptibility.

The next template process has defined steps, actions and responsibilities. You can see this theme throughout the entire information security ethos. It is all about responsibility and accountability, and then proving a certain action took place. In other words, auditing and audit trails. In information security we leave nothing to chance. You may not have the roles listed in your organisation, but you can discuss who can look after that aspect of the activity - even if it's shared between a few departments and teams, as is often the case.

STEP	ACTION	RESPONSIBILITY
1	Create and Maintain an Organisational Hardware and Software Inventory	**Asset Manager**
	• Create and maintain an inventory of hardware, OS, and major applications • Provide details about type, manufacturer, serial number, build number • Keep track of the patch level	
2	Identify Newly Discovered Vulnerabilities and Security Patches	**Vulnerability monitor**

	• Obtain timely information about components in the asset database
	  ■ Monitor mailing lists and security web-sites for available patches or vulnerabilities
	  ■ Subscribe to vulnerability tracking service
	• Match vulnerability information or patches with vulnerable systems
	• Communicate the need to patch to the Patch Supervisor or the existence of a vulnerability without an existing patch	

3	Identify patch or mitigation options	**Patch Supervisor**
	[Note: probably best to split this -> security role] • Identify patch and how to obtain • If no patch available, investigate mitigating measures: workaround, disable functionality, or other protective measures	
4	Prioritise Patch Application	**Risk Manager**
	• Assess and possibly reassess impact of the vulnerabilities • Assess countermeasures (patch, other) • Assess impact on the business • Assign an urgency level	
5	Conduct Generic Testing of Patches.	**Patch QA**
	• Obtain the patch, check integrity • Test the patch in a test environment • Report the result to the Patch Supervisor	
6	Trigger modification	**Patch Supervisor**
	• Provide a change request to change management • Indicate priority, systems, details on change, test clearance	
7	Manage the patch roll-out	**Change Management**

Step	Action	Responsibility
	Determine when to patch • Determine how to patch • Schedule change with Operations Also: • Perform Automatic Deployment of Patches (When Applicable). • Configure Automatic Update of Applications (When Applicable).	
8	Apply changes	Operations
	• Implement the Patch • Report the result to the Change Management	
9	Update status of systems	Change management
	• Inform Asset management • If problem, investigate mitigating measures	
10	Verify Patch Installation	Risk Management
	• Execute vulnerability scans or fingerprinting scans on hosts, network and infrastructure components • Inspect incident reports for causes related to missing patches • Make delta analysis of documented versus real state • (re)start change requests when necessary	

The patch process

It is also worthwhile mentioning that you will want to test the patches in a test environment, as patching can sometimes break your applications and running services. In fact, facing up to the prospect of the patch breaking the running services, is often the single biggest reason patch management and deployment is put off, put back or delayed. The delay resulting in a compromise, and ultimately a data breach.

Security bulletins should contain:

• Technical details an attacker needs to exploit the vulnerability addressed by the bulletin. For example, an attack may require physical access or the user must open a malicious email attachment.

- Mitigating factors that you need to compare against your security policy to determine your level of exposure to the vulnerability. It may be that your security policy mitigates the need to apply a patch. For example, if you do not have certain services running on your server, you do not need to install patches to address vulnerabilities in the service.

- Severity rating that assists in determining priority. The severity rating is based on multiple factors including the role of the machines that may be vulnerable, and the level of exposure to the vulnerability.

Sources for vulnerability reports

- CVE Vulnerability List

The CVE vulnerability-naming scheme is a dictionary of standardised names for most publicly known IT vulnerabilities. http://cve.mitre.org/.

- CERT/CC

  Advisories are warnings about the most critical vulnerabilities, and organisations should take steps to address these vulnerabilities immediately. CERT/CC advisories can be found at http://www.cert.org/advisories/.

- Various mailing lists: products, vendors, security organisations relevant for the installed base.

- Commercial offerings

  A great deal of vendors provide threat intelligence and vulnerability systems information. So this is also an area that can be explored; however, I started this book with the intention of staying vendor agnostic, but would encourage you to research this area.

Assess the patch

Patch QA should attempt to learn whether the patch:

- Corrects the vulnerability
- Opens an old vulnerability
- Creates a new vulnerability
- Reduces reliability
- Degrades performance
- Is incompatible with other required applications.

When to apply the patch

Before applying a patch, system administrators and/or security officer must decide whether they should install the patch directly on a production, development, or some other system. This complicated issue is influenced by numerous factors:

- Organisation's configuration management policies
- Seriousness of the vulnerability: What are the consequences of compromise? If the system is critical or contains sensitive data, then the patch should be applied immediately. This holds true even for non-critical systems, if a successful exploitation would lead to "rooting" of the system.
- Likelihood of compromise: if the vulnerability is easy to exploit, then the patch should be applied swiftly.
- Threat level of the system with the vulnerability: does the department or systems requiring patching face numerous and/or significant threats?
- Ability to temporarily mitigate the vulnerability through other methods (e.g., firewall rules, permission changes)
- Whether an appropriate system exists on which to test the patch

- Complexity of the patch
- Complexity of the production system
- Number of systems to be patched
- Experiences of others in installing the patch
- Vendor guidance (this includes all vendors whose applications are running on the systems to be patched)
- Previous experience in patching the systems on which the patch will be installed.

Process to determine urgency level

Deciding upon an urgency-level comes down to assessing the risk of not implementing the patch.
To assess this risk, evaluate:

- The probability of a compromise (feasibility in time, equipment, expertise or probability of occurrence)
- The impact of a compromise (impact on direct/indirect, tangible/intangible and operational/strategic damages for your organisation or the system)

To structure the assignment of urgency-levels within the organisation, we use the following method:

- Assign a probability factor to the exploit
- Assign an impact factor to the exploit
- Calculate the urgency-level, based on the values of potentiality and impact

Impact Factor

Assigning an impact factor depends on the impact of the system compromise to the organisation.

Impact	Description
0	No impact (the system is not vulnerable)
1	Negligible importance
2	Can cause damage to your organisation (Organisational image, financial loss, …) Example: availability problems
3	Can cause significant damage to your organisation (e.g. legal pursuits) Example: confidentiality breach
4	Can cause unrecoverable damage to your organisation (If exploited would result in major data loss of personal Information within the high risk domains)

Impact levels

Note: for a security component (e.g. firewall, authentication server) the impact is always 2 or higher.

Assign a Probability Factor

The Risk Manager

- Reads the release notes related to the patch (or the information in the security bulletin);
- Assigns a value to the probability using one of the following probability factors, taking into account the known infrastructure and server information.

Probability	Description
0	• The patch does not fix a vulnerability
1	• The patch fixes a vulnerability, and • The system (OS, DBMS, Application) is vulnerable, and • No exploit exists (or is known to exist) and • The infrastructure (e.g. firewall) blocks a possible exploit
2	• The patch fixes a vulnerability, and • The system (OS, DBMS, Application) is vulnerable, and • An exploit exists, and • The infrastructure (e.g. firewall) blocks a possible exploit
3	• The patch fixes a vulnerability, and • The system (OS, DBMS, Application) is vulnerable, and • An exploit does not exist, and • The infrastructure (e.g. firewall) does not block the exploit
4	• The patch fixes a vulnerability, and • The system (OS, DBMS, Application) is vulnerable, and • An exploit exists, and • The infrastructure (e.g. firewall) does not block the exploit

Probability level

Calculate the Urgency Level

The Risk Manager assigns an urgency level to a patch. The table below lists the possible urgency levels.

Urgency Level	Description
Non-Critical	Patch is not a security fix or system (OS, DBMS, Application) is not vulnerable Advice: plan for implementation during a later maintenance window
Recommended	Patch is a security fix, but current risk is considered low Advice: patch within a week in scheduled window
Mandatory	Patch is a security fix, real risk, no current exploit Advice: patch same day, wait for acceptable business window
Critical	Very high risk Advice: patch immediately

Patch Urgency Levels

- Based on the impact factor and the probability, the Risk Manager calculates the urgency level using the next table.

		Impact factor				
		0	**1**	**2**	**3**	**4**
Probability	**0**	N	N	N	N	N
	1	N	R	R	R	M
	2	N	R	R	M	C
	3	N	R	M	C	C
	4	N	M	C	C	C

N=Non-critical
R=Recommended
M=Mandatory
C = Critical

Calculation of urgency level

How to apply the patch

Consider:

- The cost of deploying one patch versus cost of deploying a bundle of patches;
- Automated versus manual deployment;
- Whether the patch can be consistently deployed throughout all vulnerable systems.
- Applying patches to multiple servers may seem a daunting task and especially daunting when implementing patches on hundreds or thousands of desktop systems.
- This task can be made less burdensome through applications that automatically distribute updates to end-user computers.
- Some of these patch automation tools are included with network operating system software, whereas third-party vendors distribute others.

TAKE HOME

•Patch management is a critical activity that needs strong policies and management buy in.

• Look to build staging environments to test patches before deployment to ensure that the patches do not break your live systems.

• Aim to address external critical vulnerabilities in 10 days. 52 % of data breach in 2015 were external data breaches (Source Gemalto data breach level index)

•Worrying about breaking your live systems is not a defence for not patching.

Vulnerability Management

To start this section, I would like to define the specific wording of what a vulnerability is: -

"A vulnerability is defined as an operational flaw that can have a negative impact on the confidentiality, integrity and availability of a system and/or electronic information."

The vulnerability management component forms one of the key tenets in parallel to patch management, in reducing your breach susceptibility. You should ultimately aim to deliver an automated enterprise wide vulnerability scanning system, which will be fully automated with risks ranked by the CVSS score across your organisations business units allocated to owners or department owners. Some organisations manage the number of vulnerabilities on a department basis owned by a senior manager, whose performance related pay is based upon their ability to get the number of vulnerabilities down to an acceptable level that is stated within the organisations information security policy.

The ultimate goal in the vulnerability management context is to have a clean crisp dash board, showing risk ranked by the CVSS with historical reports showing before and after scenarios. You should see the number of critical and high vulnerabilities falling or coming down, which means that your risk is moving from a high-high to a low-low i.e. High likelihood and High Impact to Low Likelihood and Low Impact.

Threats and Vulnerabilities sit together very well and we often call this whole vulnerability piece threat a vulnerability management program or TVMP.

The TVMP or in layman's terms the vulnerability scanning process should ensure: -

- Threat and Vulnerability Management is a security practice designed to proactively prevent the exploitation of IT vulnerabilities that exist within your organisation.

- The TVMP provides us with a customised framework for processing and prioritising security intelligence so we can proactively combat threats and vulnerabilities before they become incidents.

- The data used in the program is based on a Global Intelligence Network consisting of Intel feeds from various sources, such as underground hacker forums, community peers and national agencies. There should be someone in your team or organisation looking at this information round the clock.

- The expected result is to reduce the time and money spent dealing with vulnerabilities and exploitation of those vulnerabilities.

A successful vulnerability management programme needs to be coordinated and relies heavily on an asset inventory. We covered this in detail, so now you should see why asset management is critical, you can't scan and secure what you don't know.

The vulnerability management programme (VM) approach should cover the organisation's full public portfolio, as well as check for vulnerabilities on critical assets across internal networks, both from the outside-in and the inside-in. The VM Domain should track vulnerabilities for your own software too. Your applications will most probably be examined by security researchers and they will make a disclosure to you that your application contains vulnerabilities. Any organisation that sells software is generally a target for security researchers. These researchers may use the software and their skills to find holes security weaknesses and generally report this to the organisation for fame, or to raise the profile of their security consulting organisation.

Details from security researchers who find vulnerabilities in your software should be captured and reported with feedback back to the Dev team. All vulnerabilities should be catalogued and responded to within a legal and responsible disclosure centric manner. Furthermore, exploits and intelligence in-the-wild (ITW) should be collected and analysed to ensure a proactive approach is positioned to deal with your product vulnerabilities.

The next graphic depicts a typical approach of the timescales to patches that are ranked by the CVSS score. So for example anything that is between 7.0 and 9.9 is classed as a high, and is patched within 30 days if external. You may be able to bring these values down to days or hours, depending on your teams and resources to deploy for patching.

Common Vulnerability Scoring System CVSS

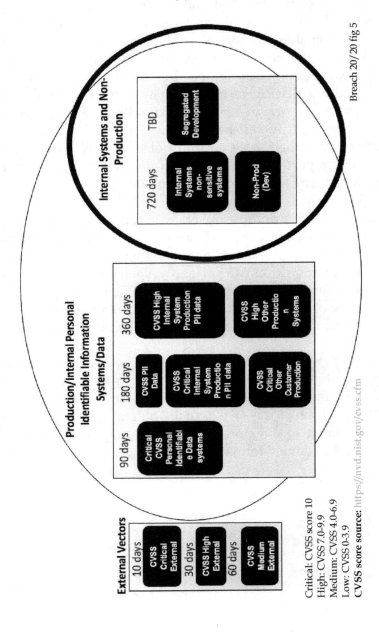

External Vectors

10 days
CVSS Critical External

30 days
CVSS High External

60 days
CVSS Medium External

Critical: CVSS score 10
High: CVSS 7.0-9.9
Medium: CVSS 4.0-6.9
Low: CVSS 0-3.9
CVSS score source: https://nvd.nist.gov/cvss.cfm

So to recap we definitely need formal ownership of someone within the organisation to deal with vulnerabilities.

The organisation is responsible for developing and maintaining a vulnerability management program to evaluate and address the company's vulnerabilities related to systems and applications used to process production information. This should be supported with information security policies to cover vulnerability management.

The Vulnerability Management Framework must be followed by all workers (employees, contractor, or 3rd parties) performing work for, and handling your projects and information. I recently did some work where there was a debate on who would deliver the vulnerability scanning. It was a simple case of pointing them to the contract that stated all deliveries from this supplier will be accompanied with acceptable vulnerability rankings and a clean report. The clean report does not mean there would be zero vulnerabilities, but that the projects would be acceptable based upon the end clients risk appetite.

We can see below a basic strategy to manage, identify, remediate, and report vulnerabilities in the following four distinct stages: Discovery, Un-Authenticated, Authenticated, and Spidering.

Don't be too worried if you don't understand all of the jargon – the premise is very straight forward – we must have a policy that states we have to remove vulnerabilities and we have tools, such as scanners that do this for us by connecting to the device over the networks and producing reports whose findings are ranked by the CVSS scores.

The following is a diagram displaying end-to-end vulnerability management process.

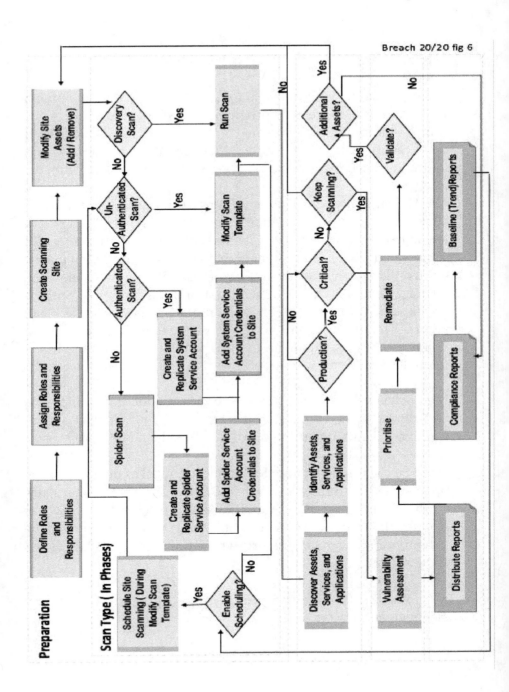

Breach 20/20 fig 6

Roles and Responsibilities

A key factor to a successful vulnerability management program is to clearly define the individuals and their roles and responsibilities.

A breakdown of potential roles is listed below that can be tweaked for your uses.

- *Information Owner* - A designated organisation employee for whom the information is being processed, transmitted and stored for:

    - Classifying the criticality of the information residing on the system – This will be covered in later chapters.

- *Application Owner* - Designated employee(s) who is/are responsible for the following:

    - The applications or programs running on the system
    - Identifying Information Owners
    - Reviewing vulnerability reports
    - Remediating application vulnerabilities according to the SLAs regarding when third parties should have had rigid guidance in the form of SLAs of when they must patch.
    - Developing remediation plans

- *System Owner* - Designated employee(s) who is/are responsible for the following:

    - The hardware, software, Operating System, and data storage of the system(s) used to process and store the information.
    - Identifying Information and Application Owners
    - Determining if the system is designated as production
    - Reviewing vulnerability reports

- Remediating system level vulnerabilities according to the SLAs
- Developing remediation plans

- *Network Owner* - Designated employee(s) who is/are responsible for the following:

  - The hardware, software, Operating System, and appliances used to transmit the information.
  - Classifying the criticality of the network
  - Determining if the network is designated as production
  - Reviewing vulnerability reports
  - Remediating network vulnerabilities according to the SLAs
  - Developing remediation plans

- *Risk Manager (RM)* – Member(s) of the (IT Information Security) team having the following responsibilities:

  - Oversite of the vulnerability management program
  - Reviewing remediation plans and assessing risk
  - Providing final approval of remediation plans and recommendations to mitigate risk
  - Reviewing vulnerability reports and trends
  - Escalating non-compliance to senior management or the risk officer and the governance department.

- *Vulnerability Assessment Administrator (VAA)* – Member(s) of the IT Information Security team having the following responsibilities:

  - Overall administration of the Vulnerability Assessment System (VAS)
  - Discovering new assets on the network and distributing reports to the Vulnerability Manager
  - Scheduling vulnerability scans by business unit

- Scheduling appropriate vulnerability and compliance reports

- *Vulnerability Manager* - Each line of business unit (LoBs) and/or function department within the organisation must identify representative(s) to act as the Vulnerability Manager (VM). The VM is the focal point for managing vulnerabilities for the business unit and has the following responsibilities:

  - Interfacing with the VAA regarding general VAS administration
  - Receiving system discovery reports and disseminating them to their respective System and Application Owners
  - Defining systems as production assets in the VAS as provided by the System Owner.
  - Assigning criticality to systems/assets in the VAS as provided by the Information Owner.
  - Prioritising vulnerability remediation (vulnerability criticality weighted against the criticality of the information, application and system respectively)
  - Assigning vulnerability remediation

In summary, the vulnerability management programme is an essential aspect to your data breach protection approach.

Get this right and you will be in a much better position than those organisations that struggle in this area due to geographic and decentralised locations, sheer size or having the wrong priority in information security.

TAKE HOME

• Once you have a near real time list of assets perform vulnerability scanning.

•Scan external systems daily

• Scan results should identify high risk systems with high CVSS scores and fixes should be prioritised.

•Perform WIFI security testing to ensure correct configuration are deployed in WIFI APs

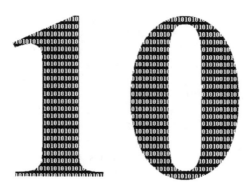

Data Classification

In the same way that we built up our story incrementally about collecting asset information and then started to perform scans to find and rank vulnerabilities, this chapter covers the recommended approach to classifying data.

It should come as no surprise to you that all data is not confidential. A newspaper is public information, but your passport and driving licence will hopefully not be left around, as they are both sensitive documents.

The Data Classification "Policy" establishes appropriate management and protection of information. It specifies how information should be handled, stored, transferred and protected from unauthorised access, modification, disclosure, and/or destruction, based on its level of criticality and sensitivity.

Whether for internal use or in conjunction with services performed on behalf of clients, client's customers and consumers' data must be classified in accordance with its criticality and sensitivity. The policy should ensure the minimum controls required to protect the confidentiality, integrity, and availability of client/customer and consumer information. The classification of information along with the corresponding security and handling requirements helps to protect information assets from unauthorised access, compromise or disclosure.

All organisational information is deemed or classified by a banding or marking, based upon the information it contains. Sounds a little long winded, but in practice it is again straightforward.

You have some information —whatever it is, is academic — that information is either *highly confidential, internal use only* or *public information*. I picked these bandings as they are quite popular but you may see some other classification headings, such as confidential, internal, public; keep it easy to start with.

This labelling means a simple thing – the information must be protected based upon how it is classified. Highly classified information when no longer required or no longer in use must be shredded in paper form and destructive deleted (overwritten multiple times) if in electronic form. On IT systems when you perform a delete function from the operating system the data appears to have been deleted and you have the free space back. In actual fact the file marker is removed but the file still resides in unallocated space, which means it can easily be recovered with forensics software. The way around this (and again it comes down to security policy) is to use a destructive delete tool, which writes over the file multiples sweep with random one's and zero's.

Corporate information is a company asset and must be protected from its creation, through its useful life and disposal. It must be maintained in a secure, accurate, and reliable manner and be readily available for authorised use.

Before applying these protective measures, we need to know what to protect. Not all information shares the same security requirements. Therefore, we need a mechanism to classify information and assets.

Information must be classified. Once it is classified, we can decide which level of protection is needed. Maybe you or someone will be responsible for the protection of the information or the asset. This is called the **Owner**. He or she is responsible for classifying the information or assets. They are to grant, or timely revoke access based on the need-to-know principle, so that information is protected from unauthorised disclosure, use, modification, and deletion.

A number of recent data breaches reported one of the key recommendations were simply to conduct a data classification review. The review was required so that the organisation could group assets based upon how sensitive the information was, and subsequently, protect that data based on how it is classified.

A key concern: The organisations that had been breached had no concept of protection mechanisms and how they related to the sensitivity of the data. Ask them the same question we covered earlier — would you leave your passport, ATM card, employment contract or salary information in a public area?

Of course not. So why were they unable to classify these data sets that were subsequently hacked or compromised? Well, at least a great number of organisations have learnt from others mistakes, and are now doing this which is great news, let's just hope yours is going to be one of them. Statistically, not many organisations experience a second data breach. The first breach is normally enough of a wakeup call.

So, information has impact on the value of the business; however, it also has:

- Strategic value

- Mandatory data for the execution of critical business processes

- Commercial value and recovery value.... sometimes when we want to understand the value of our information we can use the metric of 'how long will it take the organisation to recover from losing the information'.

At a minimum we must at least assign owners and assign levels which are based on sensitivity and business impact. Procedures for labelling and handling different levels of information, including electronic and paper transmission (post, fax, E-mail etc.) and speech (telephone or conversation) must be determined.

Users tend to over classify their own work. They seem to think that the classification level assigned to their own data reflects their own level of importance within the organisation.

As an exercise, take a view of your organisations' information flows, such as project information, HR information, and credit card data you process every day, how would you classify the below data? This is a simple table. Go ahead and assign levels from 1 to 4 (1 being the highly confidential and 4 being public information).

Classification	Data Type	Security Controls
Highly Confidential	HR Staff Record	Encryption
Sensitive	Project Information (not sensitive project but an office move).	Zipped archives with strong password and basic encryption
Public Information	Team Meal E-mails	You decide ??

You get the idea. This should be done with all your information assets. Notice the security controls section. Yes—we did say that the classification will determine how we secure the data.

The following table shows an approach for document classification. As you can see, by and large, everything that we can do with this organisation's document is based upon the classification objectives.

Mechanism	Strictly Confidential	Restricted Communication	Internal Use Only	Public
Storage	Locked cabinet, only accessible by owner or recipient	Closed cabinet Personal information: locked cabinet.		-
Access Rights	Approval by owner, need-to-know principle, timely revocation of physical access, least privilege	Local manager, need-to-know principle, timely revocation of physical access		-
Dissemination	Approval of information owner	-		-
Copying	Only after permission of and executed by the owner	No restrictions (need-to-know principle applies)		-
Faxing	See copying, do not leave the fax unattended until processed, ensure readiness of recipient, cross-check correctness of number	See copying		-
Release 3rd Parties	Approval owner, NDA agreement – High Strength Encryption only. Secure Couriers with transaction receipt to be used.	NDA		-
Labelling	All pages are to be numbered logically	All pages are to be numbered logically		Provide accurate release date, classification level "Public"
Packaging	Address to specific recipient, using double envelopes, while masking the sensitivity category on the inside envelope	Address to specific recipient, using single envelopes		-
Tracking Process	Owner must be able to present list of recipients, number of copies, storage locations, number of people that viewed the document, who destroyed the information	-		-
Disposal	Cross-cut shredding or secure disposal bins	Use disposal bins for paper disposal		-

Quick recap question - How does classifying your information reduce your data breach susceptibility?

Data Classification and labelling your information will allow you to rank your information in a way that lets you apply the correct level of security. Period. If you don't classify, you can't precisely know what controls are required to secure your information. Classification is also a key step to help you establish solid practice for asset removal and disposal. One organisation in the public domain for allowed old servers to be sold at low cost to staff members. Some staff made these purchases and a few servers ended up on an auction site only to have their disk drives forensically recovered with open source tools! Guess what was found?? This organisation has not taken the opportunity to formalise the way they dispose of assets and data destruction. What were they missing?

TAKE HOME

• Classify your data by defining what is confidential, internal and public information within your organisation.

• Use supporting policies to ensure ALL data within your organisation is classified - build security controls based upon the classification of your data.

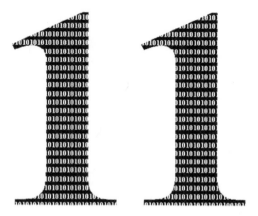

Secure by Design

The most successful breach prevention strategies that I have seen tend to be a mix of strong governance mandates, information security policies, mature processes, as well as having a focused approach on the use of tools which are selected and deployed in a methodical manner.

The approach that we should consider carefully is to attempt to deploy our security solutions within a defence in depth model, or what is known as layered security. This model, sometimes called DiD, is key to ensuring that security incidents, violations and breaches are controlled by a layer of controls with no one single tool or approach responsible for the overall strength of the security model.

The classical internet security perimeter model of firewalls, guarded by intrusion detection systems, in addition to networks for public servers (DMZs) and security zones for internal zones still exists, but with the exception of now having multiple security perimeters. These additional security perimeters allow for organisations to leverage partner network access, remote access and VPN for staff and use of cloud services with private and public cloud deployments. It's a management overhead but it does not change the requirement to adopt a layered security solution design approach.

Security solutions can help the organisation by detecting, protecting and correcting a particular undesirable security condition, such as malware, trojans and phishing attempts. The current market for security solutions is quite cluttered with hundreds, if not thousands, of products available from vendors. This then leads to the question; what solutions do we need? The answer to this question is alarmingly simple; we need approaches that may use tools to mitigate our earlier threat and risk mapping exercises. So once we understand the threat and risk landscape we can go to the designers and solution architects (who should also be aware of the threat landscape) and ask them to design a security solution that specifically mitigates defined risks.

Let's also keep in mind the basic question of how much do we spend on protection? Or, how do we split the budget for the controls? In other words, do we spend 60% of our budget on the firewall? No we don't, we look at where the biggest risks are, the value of the data and the approaches and techniques used by hackers. We then mitigate those approaches with the security solution and tools, etc. We must remind ourselves of the statement *"Cost of protection Vs. Cost of loss"*.

Naturally we will have the standard controls i.e. use of firewall, switches for VLANs, Intrusion, detection, prevention, data leakage prevention, SPAM filtering and e-mail security etc. but beyond those areas we will need to understand more about the mitigation efforts.

An organisation announced recently that they had dropped the use of anti-virus – a bold approach indeed, but not as far out as one may think. What they have decided is that it is better to deal with the effects of the malware rather than the detection. That actually works, since end-point security is absolutely key now to reducing your data breach prevention. Whilst this approach is novel we do need to err on the side of caution, and would generally only be recommend it for those organisations that have a mature security controls and a deep understanding of their threat landscape.

Defence in depth, D.i.D for short (sometimes referred to as 'the onion model'), is the security design principle of deploying multiple layers of security countermeasures, which together establish a more robust and integrated defence. Defence in depth significantly increases the workload of the attacker and can reduce the probability and impact of a successful attack.

A further advantage to the adoption of the D.i.D approach is that it is assumed that each layer has a weakness that an attacker can eventually find, so adding more layers reduces the probability that the attacker will discover and exploit all of them. D.i.D buys the security management team time –whilst the attacker analyses each layer it gives the management team more time and notice to respond.

Defence in depth is normally viewed as only layers of network security controls (firewalls, routers etc.). For this reason, D.i.D is not seen as a technical control in itself but a *'design principle'* driving the deployment of security controls.

From a data control perspective, it is essential to limit access to sensitive data to only employees with a business need to know.

Our first priority is to protect our own or clients' data depending on what role you are carrying out within the data breach prevention space. To achieve this, we apply a Secure by Design philosophy, whereby every action taken and every decision made is viewed through the lens of security. The basic premise of being Secure by Design is that cyber security has no end state: that a need for constant vigilance, scrutiny and self-improvement is essential to remain ahead of cyber threats. We should be constantly trying to improve our services and security to stay in front of the ever-changing industry threats by employing a defence-in-depth strategy by putting multiple compensating controls into place to protect clients' data from malicious activity. These combined efforts, sorted below by their purpose to prevent, detect and respond, demonstrate our approach to threat mitigation.

If you haven't already established a project management office (PMO) you should look to do this as soon as possible, or at least couple this activity within an existing departmental function if possible. The security PMO is hired to ensure security requirements are identified and documented at the outset of the project, and managed through all subsequent project phases.

Security Design Principles

Logical security controls, are deployed to support all designs, and are deployed to defend against specific threats and any attempts to exploit particular vulnerabilities. These controls can be grouped into 8 critical areas. These will vary in organisations. The following list is based upon specific challenges with the data breach space and areas that are re-occurring themes within those organisations that were actually breached.

The following design principles and practice areas are often over looked. We will expand on some of the areas in more detail, later in the book.

Security Controls within Applications themselves

- System hardening and Patching
- Defence in Depth – multiple controls/onion model, different vendor firewall layers
- Definition of logical Security Domains (bordered by firewalls)
- Specific Security Management solutions (Network IDS, DLP, Antivirus, firewalls, logging)
- Infrastructure
- Secure by design

To support the above design principles, this chapter will identify a number of security practice areas that should be adopted to support the defence in depth model.

Application security (an area that is absolutely critical to reducing your attack surface area), is now the primary target area for hackers, and a subject we will cover in a lot of detail. Hackers generally do not hack Firewalls or Network equipment instead they tend to target your applications. Again we see patterns of attacks targeting applications with organisations having little or no regard to how to secure their internet and internal hosted applications.

Secure development practices provide governance and guidance to all the development teams across the organisation, in implementing security at various stages of the development lifecycle. Your software applications must be created using secure coding practices that meet industry-accepted guidelines.

This practice area ensures the Dev team, working with the security team, develops and publishes secure coding standards and guidance to the development teams. Additionally, the use of Static Application Security Testing, manual secure code review, publish secure code education and best practices are related and essential areas the information security and development team member should address. The software security practice areas are another huge data breach prevention consideration. A great deal of compromises occurs due to insecure software processes. These processes are inevitably not tested and end up in the end code and subsequently exploited.

Static Application Security Testing (SAST) - You should ensure each application contains security controls, which are tested through a variety of means, including static code analysis and dynamic scanning. All code should be reviewed by qualified personnel (who did not perform the coding prior to the release of the code to production). Your organisation's custom software should be scanned with a top industry static scanning tool that supports rules including the Open Web Application Security Project's (OWASP), Top 10 vulnerabilities, SANS Institute/Common Weakness Enumeration (CWE) Top 25, and Payment Card Industry (PCI) rule sets.

Building sound security practices

Build and hardening procedures are critical to the end point's security model and the organisation should look to have enterprise build standards and hardening procedures for Networks, Windows, UNIX and Linux. As discussed earlier, we enforce these standards through layered controls. In general, the build process requires a series of checkpoints where validation of the key control is vetted by external groups and vulnerability scanning. These newly built devices are released into operation only after validation.

Once in operation and on the network, these devices are scanned and interrogated regularly to sustain a hardened environment. The scanning checks should include vulnerability detection, operating system end-of-life, anti-virus, anti-malware, white listing, security logging, local account compliance, and patch currency. A suitable active directory group policy should be used to facilitate centrally managed settings, like domain password policy compliance/enforcement, and the global remediation of configuration related vulnerabilities

Depending on the size of your organisation a favoured approach to data leakage is use of a data leakage prevention toolset or Data Loss Prevention (DLP)

DLP may be achieved through multiple controls employed in differing combinations across the enterprise. Examples of these controls include end-user DLP policies that restrict use of removable media, encryption of hard drives, content policies that block writing of sensitive data (non-public information, personal identifiable information and Payment Card Industry information) to removable media, controls around email services to encrypt data, and strict access controls in multiple forms to prevent unauthorised access and release of the data. The use cases for DLP may include malicious and accidental data loss.

As is the case with all information security controls, you will need standards and policies that are approved by the Security Governance office, under the direction of the senior security manager and hopefully CISO if you have one.

Desktop Protection

Desktops should be protected by different PC-based agents that monitor for zero-day attacks (newly discovered exploits without a patch), encryption, prevent installation of malicious software, prevent data exfiltration, and create forensic images. Employee Internet access should be monitored.

Based upon the data classification policy there will be some aspects of your data that are marked as highly confidential that will require encryption. Security consultants should define strategies and security architectures to further advance the protection of data with a robust, layered approach to protecting data. Encryption should be a component of the strategic layered approach and solution. Creating encryption corporate policies and encryption standards should provide policy and guidance and associated standards to ensure that the organisation's sensitive data is suitably protected through the use of encryption controls for data in motion, as well as data at rest.

Firewalls should be reviewed within all environments to identify critical elements, vulnerabilities, rules, and issues for additional refinement. Many tools exist to support firewall quality assurance and review to augment your abilities regarding rule analysis, clean up and optimisation. Any unused or legacy rules that do not comply to standards and best practices may be identified by the tool, ultimately enhancing your speed of review and refinement.

Requests for use of ports and protocols are reviewed and assessed by network security teams for appropriateness based on the business need with solid change controls practices. Certain high risk protocols/ports, should be treated as an exception request, and require additional levels of review and approval within the security organisation.

As a general principle, industry-standard firewalls should be deployed. The firewall architecture should be determined by organisation with functional responsibilities in regards to firewalls and business need. Firewalls are used to deny services that are not necessary, where appropriate. Network security zones are logically segmented via firewalls, restricting the flow of network traffic from crossing secure zones. All access points into the organisation's network, and across network zones should be controlled through a tiered firewall infrastructure.

Bastion hosts are designed purely for application/system administrative functions and therefore copy, paste and file movement are allowed by design for those administrators. They use solutions where print, cut/paste, email and other functions are prohibited or strictly limited. Bastion environments are typically limited, so that only appropriate administrators for that environment may login and utilise that specific server IT asset.

Essentially it is a jump host in to a secure environment and a standard approach to access a secure environment. In essence, to get to the zone that hosts your credit card data or HR systems, you will require an IT admin to RDP (Remote connection) to a Server in that zone and then administrate other servers, and desktops from there. He or she cannot just jump straight on to any server within that secure network.

One key approach that is often used to support D.i.D is to use RFC1918 IP address i.e. Non − routable. The address space used for these segments is not routed on the Internet. Using multiple layered controls as discussed prevents single security controls from being compromised and ultimately compromising the organisation. The network segments should all be isolated from any Internet demilitarised zone areas.

To inadvertently make a bastion host network accessible from the open Internet would require multiple configuration changes on multiple firewalls in the DMZ, as well as internal security zones, which is highly unlikely. In addition, routes would have to be advertised to the internet service providers, and routing configuration changes would be required internally.

Basically, a single mistake on a firewall or router configuration will not make the bastion network segment accessible from the open Internet, but would instead require a purposeful and conscious effort with multiple modifications to be performed by multiple teams, not a single administrator.

Obviously in a small organisation you may not have multiple teams that make changes, but even in a small organisation you need a solid change control regime.

Your production network segments should be segregated from other, non-production/internal network segments. Depending on the environment, this separation is either physical (e.g. separate physical network infrastructure), virtual (virtual local area networks, virtual routing and forwarding technology, etc.) or a combination of both methods. Tier 2/internal firewalls are also used to segregate environments.

In the case of virtualised server environments, virtual machines are only allowed to be connected to pre-defined security zones that are purposefully configured on a per VLAN basis. (Please review the virtualised firewalls approach, as not all hardware appliance firewalls offer a virtualised option) These VLANs are extended into the virtual environment using virtual switches and the VLAN tags are maintained as traffic moves between the physical and virtual network infrastructure.

VLAN trunking is handled in the physical layer; the virtual switches are essentially pass-through mechanisms. Only VLANs that are authorised and presented at the physical layer can be passed into the virtual infrastructure. Once traffic is passed into the virtual infrastructure using the VLANs defined and trunked from the physical layer, the virtual switches are used to segregate traffic between virtual machines/guests on a given host.

During the project's design, this level of security detail should be addressed within the security principles that you must define for your organisation. Everything subsequent to that must follow the defences in depth approach based on sound security principles that reflect your threat landscape and security best practice. You may need input from a network solutions architect or network security individual with skills in networking to help you define the approach and principles.

Security Monitoring

Your organisation and management should implement processes and procedures to provide for the monitoring of application access, application performance, system activity, vendor product access, Internet usage and network activity. This will help ensure anomalous activity is accurately identified in a timely manner and investigated.

Monitoring may help to indicate to you when you are being attacked or compromised on your external or internal network. In practice this requires significant investment and skills sets. Your monitoring systems and employee responsibilities should be defined to help ensure adherence to monitoring requirements. Personnel should periodically review and monitor system audit logs. The frequency of system audit log reviews is generally determined by regulatory requirements, industry certification requirements and business needs. For example, you are expected to monitor critical file system changes within the card data environment for PCI-DSS purposes.

Your organisation may need to subscribe to a service for internet egress network traffic analysis which helps identify potential intruders' activities in near real-time. The service also provides additional capabilities to detect high risk events or actionable items that may not be detected by other standard security tools, including discovering exfiltrated data attempts and command and control attempts. As well as distributed denial of service attacks DDoS.

If your organisation has the relevant teams to support proactive incident response teams for security monitoring, then that's great. From experience however, it is recommended to consider professional services from managed partners that provide incident response of their tools over a secure network.

Security Event Monitoring collects and stores systems and network device logs within a Security Information and Event Management (SIEM) solution. The solution provides correlation and cross reporting capabilities, effectively providing a better means of seeing a holistic picture of security activity. The SIEM enables you to proactively investigate security anomalies, malicious and/or out-of-policy activity, and identify potential threats for necessary triage. The SIEM team is a 7X24/365-day operation. Can your organisation support a 7X24/365 monitoring approach? This level of maturity for security monitoring is sometimes called a security operation centre (SOC).

Kill Chain

In the last chapter we introduced the concept of the defence in depth model or D.i.D; furthermore, we also looked at some technical controls, such as network segmentation and monitoring security events, as well as actual endpoint controls, such as anti-virus and malware protection.

We now need to take a look at the specific techniques of how an attack takes place within an enterprise. The method of the attack compromise, the way it moves across the organisation, the various stages of the attack life cycle and the different areas that the attack touches is called the cyber security kill chain.

The kill chain has various stages. When I am working on a data breach we always use the kill chain to find out what happened at what stage and the Who, What, Where, When and How of the incident.

There is also another excellent reason why you should understand the cyber security kill chain, which is when you understand how attacks take place you can tailor and focus your defence efforts specifically at the correct stage of the cyber security kill chain. The goal here is to focus the controls at the relevant stages that the attacks go through. Using our layered approach and tailored controls we can effectively deploy effective end point security practices within the enterprise. We can say that whilst we will make efforts to control external hacking and keep the bad guys from getting in – should they get in they will be surrounded by layers of controls and these controls will effectively isolate and restrict the attack movement.

This is a very powerful notion i.e. to concentrate on end-point controls mapped to the cyber security kill chain and that are further aligned to the Detect, Deny, Disrupt, Degrade and Deceive steps within the cyber security kill chain. We can comfortably state that our job as a security defender is much easier when we defend the internal network and stop malware movement and ultimately data movement. We already discussed use of encryption on confidential data, so that should the hackers using their myriad of tools and approaches succeed, they end up with access to our data, although that data is in essence of zero value because it was encrypted.

Feel free to ask your resident security colleagues or technical teams what stage of the security kill chain does particular security technology work at? Hopefully you will get a meaningful answer. If you don't, at least you will know the answer yourself. I would like us to get into the attack approach straight away and then we can dive deeper into the kill chain.

	DETECT	DENY	DISRUPT	DEGRADE	DECEIVE	DESTROY
Reconnaisance	Web Analytics	FW ACL				?
Weaponisation	NIDS	NIPS				?
Delivery	VIGILANT USERS	PROXY FILTER	IN-LINE AV	QUEUEING		?
Exploitation	HIDS	PATCH	DEP			?
Installation	HIDS	CHROOOT JAIL	AV			?
Command And Control	NIDS	FIREWALL ACL	NIPS	TARPIT	DNS REDIRECT	?
Action On Objective	AUDIT LOG			QOS	HONEYPOT	?

Attack Approach

Below is a description of the attacker lifecycle. It is possible that the attackers may not execute all stages of the approach as part of the breach but the approach below is in essence well recognised in incident response and forensic analysis that look to uncover the method of attack.

1. Initial Compromise – During the "initial compromise" phase, the attackers successfully execute malicious code on one or more of the organisation's systems. The initial compromise often occurs through social engineering (typically spear phishing). Drive by downloads which download Malware to your Server by simply surfing the Internet from that server's browser and thus compromising an organisation's website known to be visited by their target, or by exploiting vulnerability on an Internet-facing system.

2. Delivery - Establish Foothold – During the "establish foothold" phase, the attackers deploy tools for remote access to a recently compromised system using a Backdoor. Typically, the attacker establishes a foothold by installing a persistent backdoor or

downloading additional code to the victim system known as malware.

3. Exploitation and installation / Escalate Privileges – During the "escalate privilege" phase. Privilege escalation is often obtained through password breaking tools, keystroke/credential logging, or by leveraging privileges held by an application.

4. Internal Reconnaissance – During the "internal recon" phase, the attackers explore/enumerate the environment to gain a better understanding of the network, roles and responsibilities of users. By this stage the attackers may have the same level of access as a regular or super user/admin.

5. Move Laterally – During the "move laterally" phase, the attackers use any harvested credentials acquired to move from system to system within the compromised environment. Lateral movement methods include accessing network shares, using the Windows Task Scheduler to execute Programs and using tools, such as PowerShell and other remote access tools to interact with target systems.

6. Maintain Persistence – During the "maintain presence" phase, the attackers ensure continued access to the organisations environment. Common methods of maintaining persistence are to install multiple unrelated backdoors and remote access Trojans (RATS) gaining access to the VPN, installing web shells, and implementing backdoor code in legitimate applications and systems.

7. Mission Complete - During the " mission complete " phase, the attackers accomplish their goal by the exfiltration of your data. IE. moving data from your organisation to malicious third party sites. They will then use any maliciously deployed tools to gain persistent access to your environment when they want to day or

night. At this step the hackers in many cases have more systems than official bona fide organisation users.

	DETECT	DENY	DISRUPT	DEGRADE	DECEIVE	DESTROY
Reconnaisance	Web Analytics	FW ACL				?
Weaponisation	NIDS	NIPS				?
Delivery	VIGILANT USERS	PROXY FILTER	IN-LINE AV	QUEUEING		?
Exploitation	HIDS	PATCH	DEP			?
Installation	HIDS	CHROOOT JAIL	AV			?
Command And Control	NIDS	FIREWALL ACL	NIPS	TARPIT	DNS REDIRECT	?
Action On Objective	AUDIT LOG			QOS	HONEYPOT	?

Based upon the above attack lifecycle, we can now see the attacking party pretty much moving through the stages of the kill chain. What we need to do is to ensure that the defence in depth approach that we just discussed in detail is layered such that we have tools and approaches to:

- Detect
- Deny
- Disrupt
- Degrade
- Deceive
- Destroy

At each stage along the way while the crafty hackers have infiltrated our servers and ultimately our enterprise, we need to have the correct tools and supporting policies and processes in place to support the above mitigation.

If we mitigate the 6 D's we can disrupt the entire attack from taking place. A great many mistakes are made in this area – a huge number of organisations will deploy tools but lack the overarching mapping related to the cyber security kill chain and also lack the insight into how the attacks take place and what tools work at what stage.

To be fair some mature organisations are completely on top of this kill chain area but they tend to be the big spenders with large security budgets and world class information resources. The others just kind of adopt a security through obscurity mind set.

Building out from that point, we can then discuss the Destroy stage in terms of defensive tactics. Well we do not hack back. A highly controversial subject in its own right that comes under the guise of attribution. The position of the UK government is clear in that we do not hack organisations that have or appear to attack or compromise your organisation. If you hack back it is a criminal offence.

I am not going into the specifics of each controls mapped across the 6Ds but would like to cover one which is the Chroot Jail. This is an extremely powerful Linux security mechanism that allows admins to isolate the running process from the rest of the system. It basically stops the program from getting outside of the designated directory tree. In hacker terms it prevents the hacker's tool or exploit to move laterally, effectively containing them and denying them movement. It is a very useful method to use alongside secure shell (SSH) and other deployments. Don't forget this one. Building on this is worthy of note and often called privileged access monitoring and lock down is an extremely powerful approach to data breach prevention. This category of tools works to control accounts, access and privileges. If you have these approaches and they are working effectively you are doing well.

So the take home with the cyber security kill chain is to map your controls and tools, and end point defences against the six stages of controls, so as to reduce your attack surface area.

TAKE HOME

- Ensure that your systems operate on the principle of least privilege i.e. Your staff, customers and partners have enough access to perform their job or duty but no more.

- Look at your security controls and map them with the cyber security kill chain in mind.

- Ensure that you make extensive use of encryption and tokenisation of sensitive data. Only 4% of data breaches in 2015 were encrypted (Gemalto breach level index).

- If your data is encrypted it is useless to the hacker groups.

Cloud Security

A great number of books have been written on cloud security so a simple google will provide lists that cover the security models, best practice and design approach. There are also hundreds of technical papers and presentations that can help you understand what security concerns are inherent within the cloud services space. We won't be covering the conventional cloud security generalisations, but what we will look at is the specific cloud security concerns, as they relate to data breach prevention strategies. This chapter will look at key threats and risk, as they pertain to cloud security and those areas of concerns that appear as re-occurring security themes within the cloud data breach space.

First of all, a quick cloud recap: -

Cloud in essence has three Cloud Service Delivery Models:

1. Infrastructure as a Service (IaaS)
2. Platform as a Service (PaaS)
3. Software as a Service (SaaS)
Cloud in essence has four Cloud Service Deployment Models
1. Public
2. Private
3. Community
4. Hybrid

Depending on how the organisation wishes to consume cloud services the organisation my use a combination of the above.

Cloud services extensively use Hypervisors within virtualisation technologies, which run multiple instances of an OS (or multiple OSs) on shared hardware which can be Native or "bare metal" and that can use direct physical storage and/or virtual disks.

Cloud Threat Model concerns

- The list below comes from the ENISA -- Cloud Computing Risk Assessment:

   http://www.enisa.europa.eu/act/rm/files/deliverables/cloud-computing-risk-assessment

It is a useful document in that you should at least create mitigation for each of the risks listed below. Remember risks can be accepted, rejected and transferred. In the case of the cloud, it may be that a particular risk can be mitigated by the services provided by these activities with strong SLAs and on-going testing.

As part of your cloud on-boarding process, you would want to ensure that all the risks below are listed and detailed mitigants from the provider are given.

- Risk 1: Resource Exhaustion

- Risk 2: Customer Isolation Failure

- Risk 3: Management Interface Compromise

- Risk 4: Interception of Data in Transmission

- Risk 5: Data leakage on Upload/Download, Intra-cloud

- Risk 6: Insecure or Ineffective Deletion of Data

- Risk 7: Distributed Denial of Service (DDoS)

- Risk 8: Economic Denial of Service

- Risk 9: Loss or Compromise of Encryption Keys

- Risk 10: Malicious Probes or Scans

- Risk 11: Compromise of Service Engine/Hypervisor

- Risk 12: Conflicts between customer hardening procedures and cloud environment

- Risk 13: Subpoena and E-Discovery

- Risk 14: Risk from Changes of Jurisdiction

- Risk 15: Licensing Risks

- Risk 16: Network Failure

- Risk 17: Networking Management

- Risk 18: Modification of Network Traffic

- Risk 19: Privilege Escalation

- Risk 20: Social Engineering Attacks

- Risk 21: Loss or Compromise of Operation Logs

- Risk 22: Loss or compromise of Security Logs

- Risk 23: Backups Lost or Stolen

- Risk 24: Unauthorised Access to Premises, including Physical Access to Machines and Other Facilities

- Risk 25: Theft of Computer Equipment

So the cloud offerings are not hugely different to the security concerns for a general data centre and everyday security issues we want mitigated with a new provider by performing supplier assurance. That is correct but there are a few critical and unusual areas that we need to point out, the first of which is the orchestration tooling approach.

Orchestration is a term used within cloud for tooling, and an approach that provisions, manages, deploys and reports on the cloud services running within the cloud service provider. There are both commercial and open source offerings of cloud orchestration platforms to support your cloud activities. From a cloud security and data breach perspective it is essential that we apply the same critical thinking to this whole new cloud application and related software stacks.

The attack tree below shows attack vectors that can lead to a data breach that you must look to mitigate against. What is clear is that the cloud orchestration platform is basically an essential platform to your cloud security and cloud platforms. If you were to lose your orchestration platform by way of an attack/accident you will lose your cloud services. This should be addressed in your risk assessment for your cloud services, as we did before. i.e. map the risk to a mitigation approach and rank on the probability and impact of such an attack. So this is one risk landscape you need to consider for cloud.

A quick question: why are these risks listed below not included in the ENISA cloud threat model? The answer is due to these being technical risks and would only be understood if a deeper technical dive was carried out by the technical teams.

Let's expand on this last statement. Earlier in the book we mentioned that we must perform threat and risk analysis, as well as create living registers that document the concerns/ findings.

Quite right, but now let's ensure that as we go through the threat and risk landscape we have contributors, technical teams from the network, cloud technical teams, as well as security and governance teams involved. The greater the team's involvement, the greater you will have a 360-degree view of threats and risks.

Orchestration Attack Tree

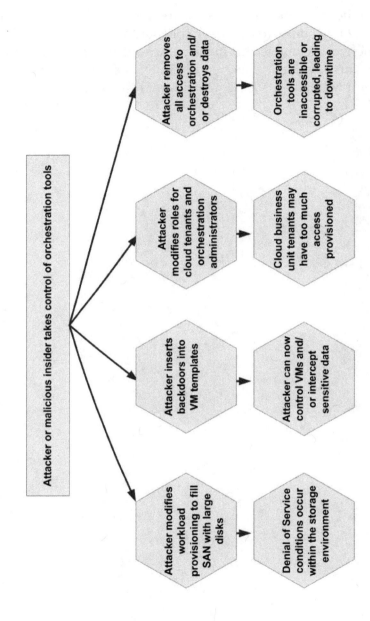

Attacker or malicious insider takes control of orchestration tools

Attacker removes all access to orchestration and/ or destroys data

Orchestration tools are inaccessible or corrupted, leading to downtime

Attacker modifies roles for cloud tenants and orchestration administrators

Cloud business unit tenants may have too much access provisioned

Attacker inserts backdoors into VM templates

Attacker can now control VMs and/ or intercept sensitive data

Attacker modifies workload provisioning to fill SAN with large disks

Denial of Service conditions occur within the storage environment

Orchestration is considered a weak point within Cloud Deployments and requires a prescriptive secure build and test approach.

Breach 20/20 fig 7

Another area in the context of orchestration is the use of open source software such as Openstack and Puppet, Chef. These tools are brilliant to use for orchestration, but they all need to be hardened with extra configurations applied and some insecure configurations removed. There are known problems with some tools, such as Django when used with Openstack web security.

You should ensure you have the relevant hardening documents that will enable you to harden your open source cloud tools.

Openstack network security allows for use of different VLANS (segments) for management VM guest network and API networks which should be used. When deploying orchestration tools to the cloud you will greatly help your data breach prevention strategies by reading the security primers on Openstack tooling.

Your cloud strategy should be coupled with a specific cloud security design document that lists all the trust zones and locations of the firewall and intrusion detection systems. It is also useful to be cognisant of the understanding that your physical firewall may not be able to handle VM-VM traffic like vMotion.

Cloud orchestration tools require considerable scrutiny both in terms of the power they afford managing the IT assets within the cloud and also from the point of view that they control your cloud services end-to-end. From a data breach perspective, there are growing concerns and attack vectors that constellate and target the orchestration platform; therefore, a deep dive in this area is a definite.

The method in which we use the cloud also needs attention – in other words forklifting: the process of taking your legacy data centre applications and uploading them in to a cloud service provider is not necessarily the best way to consume cloud services and is the expensive option to use cloud.

From a security perspective it is also dangerous. Network and Intrusion detection systems are generally not aware of API activity. Application Programme Interfaces or APIs are at the centre stage of cloud services and offer fine grain control over how the cloud services are instantiated and consumed. API security is the second big concern for those responsible for security cloud services and must be approached diligently. APIs can be secured but without detailed API monitoring cloud API end points are open by design.

Data can be leaked through third parties and the only aspect standing between a compromise of your entire virtual data centre (cloud based) is the secrecy of your API keys. Let's expand on this security concern. API access equates to physical access - how?

Traditional network security model which blocks all network traffic using host FW, remove SSH keys and passwords and install a network and monitor via agents all network traffic from source and destinations. In this scenario each and every access would hit the firewall and sensor and be scrutinised and/or captured. However, cloud using APIs allows the user which could be legitimate or malicious to snapshot the disks, mount them and extract everything without hitting the network. From this activity we will have no indication from our traditional controls that access has taken place.

Furthermore, if your APIs for your cloud environment have been exposed, your cloud environment can be used as a service to spread malware or used as a platform to launch other attacks against you or third parties.

The mitigation for API security is best practice around the end point that is using them, i.e. the orchestration platform is secured and emphasis is placed on the file shares is given with solid end point security controls, including but not limited to, application white listing, data leakage prevention and reviewing source code. This is to ensure that API keys are not hard coded. You should also make use of API key monitoring using an API monitoring tool that may be linked to your existing security operations or security event monitoring (SEM), from your cloud service provider.

Cloud metadata is another take home and can sometimes contain status scripts, which in turn contain API keys. Most cloud providers have metadata which can easily be extracted using simple WGET or Curl tools.

Some of the older vulnerabilities may be used and lead to unintended exposure of metadata. Again, the mitigation is to ensure that you're performing vulnerability scanning of your cloud environment and pushing back your cloud service provider to gain confirmation that areas have been addressed. You must cover penetration testing as well as vulnerability scanning.

Cloud API permissions are very granular and rich so locking down just the Admin function will not be sufficient enough. In fact, you will need to look at privilege chain to tie down the access across your cloud environment. In a cloud environment the change control processes can be chaotic and it is better to react to change as opposed to playing catch up. You will need change control no doubt, although experience within the cloud is that once the VMs are spun up – by virtue of the flexibility that this offers – the change control process can sometimes become difficult to manage.

The objective from a security point of view is to ensure that threats are mitigated and that the robust security controls backed up with sound cloud security policies are in-place and that you are performing regular vulnerability scanning to help you reduce you attack surface area and ultimately your data breach susceptibility. Just be prepared to be exposed to a chaotic free for all environment.

In order to mitigate the risk of API keys being exposed, we look to multi factor authentication or MFA for use extensively (and without exception) for your orchestration platform access and other incidental cloud administration access. With the MFA the user will be required to use an additional layer of security or factor for authentication, such as a token based device, an SMS message or a simple application similar to google authenticator (which is available on both iOS and Android platforms). Again, as part of the on-boarding cloud process, checks should be made to confirm that MFA is available with the cloud provider.

At the time of writing some cloud service providers did not offer MFA so that is a consideration that needs to be looked at, and will need compensation controls, such as a bastion with a second layer of authentication, or authentication gateway for use with the cloud. Due to the agility and flexibility offered with cloud services it is possible to spin up a simple virtual private cloud (VPC) instance. This is a network that can host your software and development servers if that's the approach and strategy for your organisation. The VPC Software defined perimeters can be created in seconds with new perimeters available in an instance and on demand know as software defined perimeters. Whilst this level of control and rapid deployment approach is conducive to systems migration and cloud service consumption, it also represents a specific risk if you do not have operational procedures and on-going governance on the secure use of cloud.

It is not inconceivable that a staff member would use approaches that are not sanctioned by central IT, such as opening up VPN connections from home networks and spinning up servers for testing and then accidentally shipping highly confidential data across to those servers. Thus, increasing your organisation's risk and attack surface area.

There's a growing awareness around cloud security issues caused by shadow IT, and a growing sense among enterprise information security and regulatory compliance experts that shadow IT is a problem that needs to be addressed. As we look at the next steps, we must take action to ensure that the organisation's shadow IT problem is under control. You should make sure you understand the biggest cloud security risk your company is facing. In short, it's the employees who use shadow IT.

The ultimate responsibility lies with the staff member who self-provisioned an unsecured cloud app and placed sensitive data in it. The biggest cloud security risk of shadow IT is the employee.

Employees are the ones who choose to:

- Adopt unsanctioned shadow IT applications without a clear understanding of the company's cloud data security, regulatory compliance challenges and requirements -
- Adopt unsanctioned shadow IT applications with data centres whose locations conflict with company cloud data residency requirements and policies, or that fall outside of the data movement framework i.e. UK and EU based data sets end up in foreign countries data centres', resulting in you falling foul of the data protection and GDPR the new data protection legislation.
- Copy sensitive, unencrypted, unsanctioned shadow IT applications outside of IT's visibility or control.

- Inappropriately share sensitive corporate data using shadow IT channels unmonitored by corporate DLP tools.

The above are just some of the areas that you and your organisation need to mitigate in the cloud.

Organisation that make use of cloud computing for their employees must first examine the ways that employees create cloud security risks, and find ways to prevent them from doing so. In most cases, employees adopt the use of shadow IT because they find their company's IT-sanctioned solutions not fit for purpose for their needs or too unreliable, difficult to depend on or indeed too complex to deploy.

Therefore, to help your users you need to give them the correct power but in a controlled environment, which hopefully eliminates the perceived need to circumvent the official solution. To minimise those, think again from the employee point of view. In most cases, an employee who adopts shadow IT hasn't done so to spite the IT department. In fact, most employees may not even be aware that what they're doing puts corporate data at risk. Not everyone works in the IT department after all. The sales and monitoring team aren't expected to understand the ins and outs of corporate data security and regulatory compliance. Nevertheless, perhaps these employees should receive a crash course to cover key security policy for your organisation by regular security awareness training.

Once they understand the potential consequences of adopting shadow IT, they will likely be less eager to do so. In this case, knowledge truly is power. Additionally, this is another opportunity for you to push security awareness agenda across the enterprise to communicate information security policy and related procedure, which should include secure operating models for cloud computing.

TAKE HOME

- In the cloud you still own the security of your data - your accountible

- Make use of encryption in the cloud for your data.

- Consider the use of tools for the monitoring of APIs in the cloud. APIs often bypass network security controls and allow for snapshotting of data.

- Look to develop strong on - boarding processes for cloud service providers by way of supplier assurance.

- Perform vulnerability scanning in the cloud, as well as penetration testing – with approval of the service provider.

- Make use of multi factor authentication for admin access to your cloud services.

- Monitor the usage of your clloud - unknown usage by shadow IT or malicious parties could cost you thousands in unexpected bills.

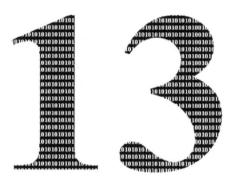

Security Testing

Security testing is another key tenet that is regularly flagged up in data breaches and is a critical activity for all projects. We saw earlier how confidentiality, integrity and availability are key information security tenets and to support these requirements we must perform security testing.

Security testing and vulnerability scanning generally work together with vulnerability scanning identifying attack surface areas via automated scans performed regularly and security testing being performed by way of penetration testing - testing external perimeters and internal networks.

We can also introduce the cyber security kill chain once again in this topic again and see both vulnerability scanning and security testing providing you with assurances that your layered security defences are operating as expected and that alarms and event triggers are being fired off to tech during the testing phases to technically prove your security defences and approach.

Red teaming is another term used to describe the security testing teams' approach in trying to compromise specific organisations' assets or services. If you have not already discussed red teaming – now would be a good time to understand how red teaming can assist your organisation by attack simulation and detailed hacker scenario walkthroughs.

Your information security policy defines the requirements to implement a risk-based testing program with consistent security testing methodology that meets legal and regulatory compliance requirements and contractual obligations, and remains current with industry trends and changes within technology.

Vulnerability and Penetration testing must be performed in accordance with the Vulnerability and Penetration Testing Standard, including requirements for testing frequency and scope. Penetration tests and vulnerability scans should be performed to detect security vulnerabilities that may lead to information technology resources being compromised. Data breach reporting and forensic reports often call out the fact that little evidence of vulnerability scanning or penetration testing was performed leading up to a particular data breach.

Network vulnerability scanning should be scheduled as part of the 'business as usual' scheduling and tasks on a monthly basis, for both internal network scanning and external network scanning.

Application penetration testing should be performed periodically against all your organisation's externally hosted assets, Internet facing, web-based applications. From a regulatory perspective if you are subject to PCI-DSS standards and reporting, then you are required by the regulator to perform annual penetration testing and quarterly scanning (external as well as internal). The regulations applicable to your sector i.e. finance, retail and government may mandate varying scanning and security testing schedules as well as the level of testing required.

You should aim to perform network vulnerability scans against all segments of your infrastructure from sources both internal to the network, and outside the network's perimeter.

Network vulnerability scanning scope is based on, but not limited to asset inventory, which you should now be on top of. This should also include external infrastructure asset inventories.

Please be aware that penetration testing and vulnerability scanning require an explicit approach from your internal management teams, external cloud service provider or any third party. Without approval in writing, your security testing and vulnerability scanning basically amounts to a hacking attempt.

Network vulnerability scanning should include the following suggested approach, but may be tweaked to your particular enterprise.

- Network vulnerability scans must be performed against all segments of your network.
- Vulnerability scanning must be conducted at a minimum frequency of a monthly scan on internal assets and weekly on external facing IP addresses.
- Scope of network scanning is defined by, but not limited to, assets listed in the asset inventories. Scope is generally validated on a weekly basis.
- Results of internal and external vulnerability scanning must be reported to the appropriate stakeholders for the remediation of identified vulnerabilities.
- All identified vulnerabilities must be tracked through remediation by the Lines of Business or departmental/divisional managers.
- Validation of remediation by the testers must (internal security consultants) must be conducted before vulnerability can be considered fully remediated. All vulnerabilities must be remediated according to the CVSS (severity level) of the discovered vulnerability.

Remember the objective is to identify vulnerabilities and their remediation by timely path management.

Application Penetration Testing

In order to identify critical actions and the thinking required to mitigate against data breaches, there are a number of approaches used. One such approach that is often seen is use of MoSCoW. This means that controls:

- **M**ust have
- **S**hould have
- **C**ould have
- **W**ould have

MSCW (known and pronounced as **MoSCoW**)

You will see Moscow used a lot in the next few chapters so a crystal clear definition of how important a control is.

Application penetration testing must include the following:
Suggested approach but may be tweaked to your particular enterprise.

- Application penetration testing must be performed at a minimum annually against all hosted, Internet facing, web-based applications.
- Frequency and Scheduling should be determined based on risk as determined by the Information Security department or advise from the security consultants.
- All applications tested as part of Application Penetration Testing engagements MUST be entered in asset database inventories as part of the asset management policy.
- Application penetration testing must be performed either against Production, or in a test environment that exactly replicates production, sometimes called staging.
- Results of application penetration testing must be reported to the appropriate stakeholders for the remediation of identified vulnerabilities.

Network Penetration Testing

Network penetration tests should be performed at a minimum annually against the organisations network or a system infrastructure change. Cloud services from sources internal to the network and sources outside the network perimeter. All infrastructure tested as part of Network Penetration Testing engagements **SHOULD** be entered in the asset inventory as this is what will be used to ensure that the scan is covering the correct network. Data discovery tools we covered in the vulnerability scanning section earlier in the book may be used. Data hives or repositories identified should also be added to the asset management database. Assessments are scoped to target high value and high risk assets as identified through vulnerability scanning. The outcome/results of network penetration testing must be reported to the appropriate stakeholders for the remediation of identified vulnerabilities.

The results of network penetration testing must be reported to the appropriate stakeholders for the remediation/correction of any identified vulnerabilities.

Data contained within vulnerability scanning results is highly confidential as the results will list potential system weaknesses. Hence application security testing and penetration testing data should be identified as highly confidential and encrypted and shared on a need to know basis only. Obviously release of this information into the wrong hands (including competitors) is disastrous and yes, it does happen.

Application Security

Application Security is another huge area that deserves a chapter of its own. A great many data breaches occur due to inherent application security flaws. Application security designs are now at centre stage in relation to risk reduction strategies, for the simple reason that there is an increased growing risk of hackers now targeting the application security, specifically web applications. Secure software does not happen by itself and requires a consistent applied methodology across your organisation. Methodologies that conform to stated policies, objectives and principles.

Your organisation should look to create and distribute an application security framework to provide application teams with a series of specific actions designed to help produce secure applications.

This is only a suggested approach, and many exist. The application security frameworks must be supported by effective tooling using security testing software to cover dynamic, as well as, static security testing.

The whole application security piece is an area that is a difficult area to get right within the security space. We have developers who can write great code and we have security specialists who can guide on security vulnerabilities. We need to marry these two roles up into a conduit that shares information in both directions. We also have at our disposal excellent baselines and security checklists, such as OWASP **www.owasp.org** that provide a wealth of application security hardening and improvements plans.

One of the key challenges in application security is to map security requirements, policies, and best practices to an application's specific architecture. Much of the framework is devoted to guiding teams through this mapping process by prescribing a well-defined course of analysis that views software in terms of threat exposure and risk.

The following is an overview of a template application security framework that you may use. It covers how to use the framework, and specifies general application security requirements.

The application security framework can be embedded within your SDLC approach which will hopefully lead to a secure SDLC or S-SDLC. Working with your developers and security consultants you should at least ensure that the framework consists of the following areas:

- Security Checkpoint Checklist
- Application Security Training Plan
- Attack Surface Analysis
- Security Model
- Threat Model
- Defence Plan
- Security Testing Plan – which should include the function and non-functional security testing requirements.

The above suggested approach which will comprise of the framework are meant to be tools and are not ends-in-themselves. A team may capture and analyse the relevant security information in a different format. The frameworks presented here as a target approach to support secure SDLC are actually based on recommendations and post-breach analysis.

These frameworks should be used by your software developers without delay, as application security and risk reduction are high profile weaknesses across development teams and recurrent themes, which can be exploited by hackers and lead to a data breach.

Hack resilient software is one that reduces the likelihood of a successful attack and mitigates the extent of damage if an attack occurs. A hack-resilient application resides on a secure host (server) in a secure network and is developed using secure design and development guidelines, as well as coding standards. Application or Software security must be addressed across the tiers and at the multiple layers that we spoke about earlier i.e. (DiD). A typical model that we use to host an integrated Web application is the 3 tier model that consists of a Web App and Database layer. A weakness in any tier or layer makes your application vulnerable to attack.

We also need to know when and how the code breaks. The scope of the domain would be more focused on securing the application. The security framework shows the processes involved during the design phase of SDLC, such as threat modelling, which provides a structure and rationale for the security process and allows you to evaluate security threats and identify appropriate countermeasures. Software security must be holistic, i.e., it must not only secure the application (software) but also secure the hosts and the network in which the software resides. Additionally, holistic security takes into account the people, the process and the technology aspects to secure applications to be deployed on secure hosts within secure networks.

Use Cases

From a data breach prevention perspective, it is recommended that project teams use as much of the framework as possible, resource constraints often make this difficult to achieve. These use cases, identify different risk classes of applications or application enhancements and specify the minimum framework requirements for each class.

The table below shows the risk classes based on whether the application or enhancement is accessible to the internet and the security categorisation of the information it handles.

	Public	Confidential	Highly Confidential
Not internet accessible	Low risk	Moderate risk	High risk
Internet accessible	Moderate risk	High risk	High risk

"Not Internet Accessible" means that the application resides in your internal network. "Internet Accessible" means that the application resides in our external network.

The scope of the security process should match the scope of the project or enhancement in most cases. Where possible, enhancements to unsecured legacy applications (applications which have not been through this process), should attempt to include more of the application's functionality, which are strictly defined by the enhancement's scope.

The minimum requirements for each of these risk classifications are listed below.

- Low Risk Applications or Enhancements
- Security Checkpoint Checklist: Complete in full.
- Security Training Plan: Complete as necessary.
- Attack Surface Analysis: Complete in full.
- Defence Plan: Complete the following:
  - Incident Contact Information
  - Response Plan for shutting down the application
- Test Plans: Complete the following:
  - Attack Surface Testing
  - Defence Plan Testing (Response Plans only)
  - Moderate Risk Applications or Enhancements
- Security Checkpoint Checklist: Complete in full.
- Security Training Plan: Complete as necessary.
- Attack Surface Analysis: Complete in full.

- Security Model: Complete in full.

Threat Model: Complete the following:
- Analyse threats against data flows of sensitive information
- Analyse threats against components which store sensitive information
- Analyse threats against authentication and authorisation components

Defence Plan: Complete in full:
- Specify events for possible unauthorised disclosure of sensitive information
- Specify events for failed logins and locked accounts
- Specify events for unauthorised access attempts
- Response Plan for shutting down the application

Threat Model: Complete in full; emphasise the following:
- Analyse threats against data flows of sensitive information
- Analyse threats against components which store sensitive information
- Analyse threats against authentication and authorisation components

Defence Plan: Complete in full; emphasise the following:
- Specify events for possible unauthorised disclosure of sensitive information
- Specify events for failed logins and locked accounts
- Specify events for unauthorised access attempts
- Response Plan for shutting down the application

Engaging the Application Security Team

One of the goals of the Application Security Framework is to empower application teams to function fairly autonomously with regards to application security. The necessary touch points are kept to only a handful, and the check points where actual approval is required are minimal. However, the team is always available to answer questions, help with cases not covered by existing policy or standards, or provide security subject matter expertise.

To meet this goal, it is necessary to identify someone on the project as the project security lead within the project management office, the PMO, as we discussed earlier. This lead should be a senior technical person. Whilst this person need not be dedicated to only security, security should be included as a significant portion of his or her responsibilities.

The expectations for the project security lead are:
Understands security and privacy requirements and is responsible for ensuring that the requirements for security, privacy and best practices are identified and implemented throughout the project. Provides technical expertise on the Application Security Framework and related security tools and methods. Acts as the primary liaison between Information Security and the project team, and escalates security related questions and issues to the appropriate Information Security specialist.

The application security team provides a security assurance manager to the project. This person works with the project security lead to help with questions, policy clarifications, and exceptional cases. This person also reviews key project documents for general alignment with application security policy and standards (we rely on the project security lead to ensure that the project's low-level details also meet security policy and standards).

The expectations for the project security lead are:

Understands security and privacy requirements and is responsible for ensuring that security and privacy requirements and best practices are identified and implemented throughout the project. Provides technical expertise on the Application Security Framework and related security tools and methods. Acts as the primary liaison between Information Security and the project team and escalates security related questions and issues to the appropriate Information Security specialist.

When a project begins its security process (preferably during the Select phase), it should assign a project security lead. The lead should then inform the application security team that the project is underway. The lead and assigned assurance manager will then begin applying the framework to the project.

General Security Requirements

This section lists the high-level, general security requirements that are applicable to most applications. Translating these high level requirements into application specific security controls is the goal of the framework.

- Complete the design analysis, test coverage, and defence plan as per the Application Security Framework
- Grant access to resources only after authenticating the requestor and confirming that the requestor is authorised for the type of access requested. This applies to both users and program components.
- Check authorisation as close to the access as possible
- All uses of passwords (including passwords for program-to-program access) must adhere to your organisations Password Policy

- Log access to sensitive information and protect the integrity of the logs – You may need to provide advice on where the logs will be stored and where they are created in industry standard formats to allow them to be integrated into a commercial grade logging solution.
- Log events which may indicate a security breach and define plans for detecting and handling an application breach
- Encrypt Confidential data as it transits the network, as per the Data Protection Policy
- Encrypt Confidential and Highly Confidential data when it is stored (including in temporary files), as per the Data Protection Policy
- Delete sensitive information that has exceeded its retention period
- All program components must run with the least privileges necessary
- All program components must fail securely
- Security controls should be layered so that if one fails there is a backup
- Applications must adhere to the organisation's coding standards
- Error messages returned to users must not reveal any details of the application's structure or operation
- Remove all unnecessary code
- Filter all input and only accept that which matches a well-defined profile of what is acceptable
- Filter all output to ensure that it matches a profile of what is acceptable
- Escape any non-alphanumeric characters which must be accepted (especially those that contribute to SQL injection, cross-site scripting, or other known vulnerabilities)
- Do not base access control or trust decisions on user-supplied information

- Use parameterised queries (bind variables) when passing parameters to SQL and do not use string concatenation
- Scan code for vulnerabilities using automated tools
- Verify that the application meets security policies and these requirements
- Verify that the application's security controls operate correctly
- Verify that the application resists common attacks such as OWASP
- Include the use of vulnerability assessment tools when testing application security

Advanced application security

The next few sections describe how to use the various key security attributes within the Framework.

Attack Surface Analysis

The concept of an application's attack surface should be detailed in your Application Security Policy. The goal of this analysis is to identify each of the application's entry points, understand the specific risks each poses, and specify the appropriate controls to filter and sanitise the input. Entry points include any input that the application accepts. Command line options, web or GUI forms, configuration files, database reads, and cookie access are all types of application input. The analysis not only identifies controls that an application must implement, but also gives guidance to quality assurance staff as to what their test data will need to look like.

- Component – in which component does this entry point exist
- Entry Point – uniquely identify the location of the entry point in the application; include its name if appropriate (as in a web form)
- Description – the type of entry point: database read, web form GET or POST, SOAP request, cookie read, etc.; include information if the point of entry is directly accessible to a user or is in some way hidden
- Defence Controls – what techniques are used to mitigate attacks through this entry point; whitelist sanitisation, encoding, and SQL parameterisation types of defences
- CMD – is this input used in a command line argument or otherwise used to invoke another program; if 'yes' then pay particular attention to possible command injection attacks
- HTTP – is this input displayed or used at a later time on a web page; if 'yes' then pay particular attention to possible cross-site scripting attacks
- SQL – is this input used as part of a database query or command; if 'yes' then pay particular attention to possible SQL injection attacks
- Security Tokens Mobile Applications–Mobile Application Security is another area that deserves a full book regards security best practice but we discuss a potential use of secure tokens that should be looked into.

Use of single sign on and use of OAuth is outside the scope of this book but if you are developing applications that use tokens you must ensure that architecturally the approaches used are tested from a security perspective to avoid replay attack and to include, Spoofing, Tampering, Repudiation, Information Disclosure, Denial of Service and Escalation of privileges. – i.e. The STRIDE threat model.

By completing the Security Model, the application team will gain a solid understanding of what information their application handles and who and what may access that information. This knowledge is critical in order to accurately specify and test the application's access controls and ultimately reduce the attack surface areas which may be targeted and lead to a data breach. As is often the case. It is anticipated that your Dev team will create the following tables:

The first table, the "Information Inventory," tracks the information handled by the application. The columns are:

- Information Item – the information handled by the applications
- Security Category – as per Information Security policy, Public Knowledge, Confidential, or Highly Confidential
- Owner – the business owner of the data
- Retention Period – how long will the data remain in the system
- Location – where in the system will the data be handled or stored; include all locations even if only used temporarily (such as in a temp file)

The "Application Principals" table lists the entities, which will access the application and the information handled by the application. The columns are:

- Principal – the entity accessing the application or data (could be a user or another program)
- Authorisation Group – the group or role to which the entity belongs
- Description – what is the entity's business function and other comments

The "Access Matrix" table ties together the previous two tables. For each information item, each principal, which needs access must be listed along with the type of access. If a principal is not listed for a particular item or a particular access is not listed for a principal, then the application must not allow access. Only accesses specifically listed in the Access Matrix are permitted.

The columns of this table are:

- Information Item – the information under consideration
- Principal – the entity which has some access to the information item
- Access Privileges – the types of access the principal is permit in relation to the information item. The basic access types are read and write, although many systems have more detailed access categories such as select, create, delete, insert, and update in databases

The "Authorisation Group List" table summarises the groups or roles specified by the application. These groups might be Active Directory groups. Typically, when an application checks to see if a user is authorised for a particular access, it checks to see if the user is a member of a permitted group. The columns are:

- Authorisation Group – the name of the group
- Location – The system, which manages the group, could be Active Directory
- Description – the business purpose of this group and other comments

Threat Model

Securing an application requires that you understand which threats could be deployed against your application. The threat model is the primary tool for gaining this understanding perhaps by using an Attack Tree. While attack surface analysis and security modelling deals with rather well known and common security concerns, threat modelling approaches security from a wider perspective and considers less common or novel threats.

The first component of the threat assessment is a description of the potential adversaries or attackers. While most people immediately think of attackers as external intruders, strong application security must also consider the existence of malicious insiders, such as disgruntled employees. The Adversaries table is seeded with common adversaries, but it will most likely require refinement for each application.

A set of up-to-date data flow diagrams (DFD) will make your threat modelling much more effective. A DFD illustrates each significant process, data store and user, and shows the information flows between them. Boundaries between processes running on different machines can be shown (and should be, especially if they reside in different network zones). Colour can be used to indicate if a particular item handles sensitive information.

Component Security Analysis

In the Component Security Analysis, you describe the risks and baseline security controls for each object in the DFD. Start by listing all of the objects in the left-most column. The Risk Type column lists the basic categories of security breaches. They are:

- Confidentiality – an unauthorised entity reads information, particularly sensitive information. The Security Model worksheet, created previously, should be consulted to understand where sensitive information is located.

- Integrity – information is created or altered by an unauthorised entity.
- Availability – information or processing is rendered unavailable for use; examples include denial of service attacks or outright deletion of information.
- Authentication – an entity masquerades as some other entity.
- Authorisation – an entity gains additional access authorisation.
- Auditability – an unauthorised entity alters the audit record or otherwise causes it to be incorrect.

The Risk column summarises the consequences should a threat of a given type be realised. "Disclosure of sensitive customer information," "alteration of financial data," and "deletion of sales records" would be valid entries in the Risk column.

In the Prevent/Detect Controls column, describe what security mechanisms are in place to mitigate the identified risk. It might be worthwhile to simply name and number the controls in the column and detail them outside the table. Since controls will often be used in multiple components, this practice helps keep the size of the table conducive to a quick examination. As you specify the baseline controls, consider the following questions:

- How does this object protect the confidentiality of the information it handles?
- How does this object protect the integrity of the information it handles?
- How does this object protect the availability of the information it handles?
- How does this object protect its own availability?
- How does this object identify the other objects or users who interact with it?

- When this object receives a request or command, how does it verify that the issuing user or object is authorised to make the request?
- How does this object preserve the integrity and confidentiality if applicable for the audit record tracking its behaviour?

When specifying a security control, include or refer to any relevant policy or compliance requirements. For instance, we have policy and compliance requirements to protect credit card numbers. If an application component stored credit card numbers, then the control specifications should indicate that it meets the High Confidentiality requirements of the Data Protection Policy. Over time, an index mapping common risks to approved and standardised controls should be developed. This library of technologies and security patterns will further streamline risk analysis.

If the control is of the detect variety, then a security event and alert should be specified. Ensure that this is identified in the Threat Model and in the Defence Plan.

Finally, the Impact indicates the degree of potential damage should the specified security control fail. If the organisation or the organisation's customers would be significantly harmed by a breach of the specified type, then the impact is high. Similarly, note cases where moderate or little harm would be done, as moderate or low impact.

Threat Modelling

Now that the risks and baseline controls are understood for each object the application is comprised of, it's time to turn to modelling the actual threats. Our basic approach is to consider each object in the security analysis (start with those with a high impact) and determine how adversaries might circumvent the specified security controls. Each such circumvention is a possible threat and is a candidate for additional countermeasures.

Threats in this framework have the following eight characteristics:

- Threat Objective: What security breach occurs if this threat is realised?
- Scope: Which objects in the component analysis are affected by this threat?
- Adversary: Who can carry out this threat in terms of capabilities and access?
- Threat Vector: What mechanism will the adversary use to realise the threat?
- Scenario: What steps are involved in realising the threat?
- Countermeasures: How will the threat be mitigated?
- Extensions: How might this threat be extended or interact with other threats?
- Severity: Given the countermeasures, how likely is this threat?

Within the threat model, organise threats by object. This will make it easy to review later to ensure that each object in the DFD is fully covered.

Threats might be very similar, but will differ at the very least in the scenario and scope. If two threats have the same scenario, then they should likely be combined into a single threat with multiple adversaries.

Defence Plan

Should an attack target your organisation's application, procedures must be in place to identify the attack and respond as necessary to protect your information assets. An application's Defence Plan forms the basis of this functionality.

Defence begins with logs of security events the application encounters. The Event Catalogue lists and describes these events.

- Event Name: the name of the event
- Event Class: the type of event
- Description and Triggers: the event's meaning and the conditions which trigger the event
- Event Specifics: information about the event itself such as application response, principal, application state, etc.
- Log Location: where is the event logged

The Significance and Alerting table describes how each event class should be prioritised and handled. Note that the plan allows many events in the event catalogue to belong to the same event class, but this is not necessary.

- Event Class: the type of event
- Significance Criteria: when is an event of the indicated class tagged with a High, Moderate or Low significance (significance is tied to the how long the event must remain in the log record)
- Alert Criteria: often isolated events are not a cause for concern but are when correlated with other events; such correlation criteria should be listed here
- Responses: what should be done when an alert from this event class is generated

The specific instructions for each type of response are detailed in the Response Plans section.

- Response: a short phrase identifying the response
- Description: what does this response accomplish

This entire section has been expanded to provide you with a detailed subject matter breakdown of one of many approaches to improve your application security and build a secure SDLC. By working with your developers and counterpart security colleagues that may be supporting the development function, you can adopt similar approaches. By doing so, these will ensure you have end to end coverage allowing you to remove software vulnerabilities that may be exploited during live hosting on both internal and external internet facing services.

We occasionally hear a mind-set that if you have a good application firewall then you need not build secure software. Well this train of thought is flawed, because application hooks can be exploited to circumvent application firewalls masquerading in genuine regular traffic and sometimes being encrypted making the firewall effectively blind to what the traffic contains.

An important area for you to read more on is the specific threat and mitigations for application security which will help you cover the latest techniques used by hackers and exploits in the wild, aimed at application level attacks to include, Spoofing, Tampering, Repudiation, Information disclosure, and Denial of Service and escalation of privilege or STRIDE.

In the meantime, it is essential that you take a serious look at your SDLC approach with a fine tooth comb and adopt a risk based approach.

Hackers target the software environment (applications). Gartner publications indicate that 70% or more of attacks are in the application layer. In addition to functionality, other factors such as compliance to regulations and privacy requirements need to be incorporated into the software because non-compliance to these requirements can have serious detrimental consequences. Additionally, security has been traditionally bolted on instead of being built into the software development life cycle and so is not comprehensive.

In today's computing world, the software is an integral part of the system and in some case, such as Software as a Service (SaaS), the software is the system itself. The main driver for secure software development is the protection of the brand or reputation, and the cost of a security breach can be extremely damaging to the corporate brand.

TAKE HOME

• Perform security testing at both network and application levels.

•Hackers are now increasingly attacking application weaknesses so static application security testing (SAST) and dynamic application security testing (DAST) are essential practices.

•If you have the opportunity perform red team exercises. This is where teams authorised in your organisation will try and infiltrate systems.

•Perform mock testing – or incident simulations – you will learn a great deal by walking through the steps as though you have experienced a data breach.

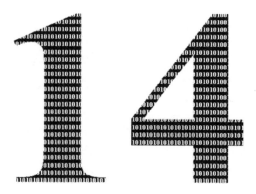

Supplier Assurance / Due Diligence

Supplier assurance when outsourcing your organisational assets, whether that be via a managed service to support a security operations centre, a card processing outlet, such as a business process outsourcing (BPO) or consuming cloud based services is critical.

We have discussed security approaches and essential security actions to reduce your breach susceptibility from the organisations' points of view. We also need to examine external partners and the supplier assurance function. Supplier assurance is the process of ensuring that the suppliers that are engaging with your organisation are fit for purpose to support your business. By using audit processes and questionnaires as well as on-site reviews, we must ensure that the delivery partner is financially stable, and that they are hiring staff with solid background employment checking procedures and criminal checks. Subsequently, we move into the actual way the external partner is managing your data and storing, processing and de-commissioning it, if and when this is required.

A useful question to ask your external partners is that should they experience a data breach - will they inform you? will they let you know that data has been compromised on a bleak Tuesday afternoon at 3 pm? A great number of providers will not actually inform the end client if they experience a data breach. So please check this area and ensure that suitable legal agreements enforce data breach notification requirements with strong SLAs between you and the third party supplier.

Generally, this supplier assurance activity falls into the governance space which performs these sorts of checks and they may need your technical security assistance by requesting a breakdown of the technical security requirements you would expect from the supplier. As a starting point, your information security policy should have explicit requirements to regularly check third party suppliers before you do business with them.

Ongoing checks and audits should then take place to ensure the suppliers are doing what you expect from them. You will also need to request the supplier's information security policy to ensure that it has sufficient coverage and is aligned to best practice. Copies of sanitised security testing, such as vulnerability scanning and penetration test results, should be requested but be prepared to get stone walled with a blanket refusal that the supplier does not share sensitive internal information with the end clients due to a multi-client environment. What they may and often claim is that by sharing the security testing information with you, they are actually sharing vulnerabilities that may just not be applicable to you but their other valued clients.

If your third party supplier takes this stance you may wish to request sanitised reports – which has the IP information removed but simply shows that no critical or high vulnerabilities with a CVSS score that is high i.e. 7.0-9.9. In this regard you will also want to consider having your contract and SLA cover what level of detail the supplier assurance function is provided with. For example, contractors committed to perform quarterly audits of the supplier.

As part of your information security policy, standards and guidelines you should at least develop Supplier Security Standards which are comprised of the following five requirement levels:

• Network-level requirements
• Operating system-level requirements
• Application-level requirements
• Data-level requirements
• General requirements

The supplier should respond in writing, using your requirements by completing the Supplier Security Review Checklist. If the supplier is not compliant with a specific requirement, but has implemented a similar compensating control, the supplier should explain this. Below are areas that you should look into for your suppliers to rate their ability to host your data or services.

You should aim to ensure that all requirements must be implemented as a condition of service before going live, unless explicitly specified otherwise in your supplier assurance referenced in your standards.

The supplier must satisfy these requirements prior to any engagement with your organisation. The requirements are broken down further for you to use as a start for the security policy and supporting procedures.

Network-Level Requirements

The supplier must have a security program in place that comprehensively addresses network-level requirements

• The supplier must use International Computer Security Association (ICSA) Labs or a Trust Technology Assessment Program (TTAP) certified firewall to protect servers hosting your information. EAL certified Firewalls are also relevant here.

• The supplier must specify the name and version of the firewall(s) used.

• The supplier must submit a sanitised network diagram for the portion of its network used to supply services to your organisation.

Intrusion detection

• The supplier must use a network-based intrusion detection system (IDS) to monitor the segment (son servers hosting your information, which are logically located. Host intrusion prevention systems (HIPS) should also be considered for servers.

This requirement should be implemented within six (6) months of contract signing date.

• The supplier must specify the name and version of the network-based intrusion detection system (s) used.

Your asset management process and asset inventory must include all of the assets you use with a managed service provider, or cloud service provider. You own these assets and from an attack surface area, vulnerability testing and penetration testing perspective, the same concerns exist as your on-site assets i.e. How will you test, patch and comply with effective patch and build standards if you don't know what assets you have? It makes no difference whether the assets are being managed by a third party or by your organisation in-house. What are the lines of demarcation? Who is doing what? Are they patching or are you? Are they testing or are you? Remember – you can outsource the pain and the infrastructure but you cannot outsource your accountability – you will always own the risk.

Vulnerability assessment

This area has been covered in detail in previous sections – you must perform vulnerability scanning on your networks and so must the third party that holds, processes and transports your data.

• The supplier must use commercial products or freeware (e.g., Nessus) for vulnerability assessment and/or penetration testing of the segment(s) on which servers hosting your organisations information are logically located.

• The supplier must specify the name and version of the network-based vulnerability assessment tool(s) used.

• The supplier must conduct vulnerability assessment and/or penetration testing at least twice a year. Regulatory requirements may mandate that penetration testing be performed in different cycles such as monthly.

• The supplier must submit the vulnerability assessment and/or penetration testing report(s) to your Information Security department upon request.

Operating System-Level Requirements

• The operating system(s) for the supplier's servers must be hardened prior to use, in accordance with recognised best practice configuration(s). These operating system(s) for servers must not be operated with an out-of-the-box configuration. Several organisations and suppliers have documentation, checklists or tools designed to facilitate this security configuration process, and are generally recognised as best practices.

• For each platform used to host your information, the supplier must indicate whose guidelines it adheres to regarding operating systems best practices (e.g., operating system supplier, Centre for Internet Security).

• The supplier must submit documentation related to their patch management program in place.

Application-Level Requirements

●For Technology Service Approval Only: The following programming languages must not be used for the application(s) hosting the service(s)

Not to be used for application(s) hosting the service(s)
Visual Basic (VB)
PHP
Perl
Python
Django with Openstack for Cloud without detailed evidence of hardening being in place.

Nb. The above list is not exhaustive and you must call out software that is generally not used within your organisation for security concerns, including but not limited to, end of life software concerns (no security patches being developed by vendor), security problems with a lack of support of encryption etc. This information would normally be referenced in your information security policy as recommended application architecture.

These high-level languages provide limited controls and checks for important aspects of an application, including advanced data manipulation, programming structure, and security features and operating system resources, such as memory and processes. Generally, these languages are not used for applications with specialised or granular functions due to their limitations.

•Secure Programming Specifications are provided for the following categories. The supplier must state their compliance level against these specifications and provide further information upon request.

Logical layers of the application architecture

•The supplier must provide documentation on overall architecture, development and implementation of application(s) used by your organisation. If application-level security is applicable, the supplier must meet the related security requirements.

•The supplier must submit documentation on an application patch management program with version control.

•Vulnerability assessment/audit

•The supplier must use commercial products or freeware for vulnerability assessment and/or penetration testing of the installed application(s) providing information.

•The supplier must specify the name and version of the application-based vulnerability assessment tool(s) used.

•The supplier must conduct vulnerability assessment and/or penetration testing at least twice a year.

•The supplier must submit the vulnerability assessment and/or penetration testing report(s) to Information Security upon request.

•The supplier must engage an independent and reputable IT company to audit their code. The subsequent audit report must be approved by your IT security group before going live.

Data-Level Requirements Controls

•Protection and privacy of personal information

•The supplier must use strong encryption for transmission of personal information collected from your organisation.

•If your organisation completes Web-based forms with the supplier and enters personal information, the supplier must protect that session using Transport Layer Security (TLS) or a Secure Sockets Layer (SSL, version 3.0). The supplier must support both TLS 1.2 or above and SSL v3.0 as the minimum requirement.

•The supplier must use strong encryption (i.e., $\geq$ 256-bit symmetric) to encrypt and store personal information.

•If the supplier receives personal data from your organisation, it must be explicitly acknowledged. All data elements must be fully identified, with a clear explanation regarding the need and how the information will be used.

•The supplier must provide session encryption to protect authentication information (e.g., username + password) when your personnel logon to a server (e.g., to upload content, or to perform any administrative function). This session encryption may be SSL or Secure Shell (SSH). The supplier may not use insecure means for logon (i.e., username + password transmitted in the clear).

•To ensure authenticity and integrity, the supplier must have the capability of digitally signing messages sent (e.g., e-mail, newsletters) on your behalf or to you.

•The supplier must provide dataflow documentation highlighting the type of data involved at each point of the application system and how it is secured, if not already addressed in the earlier requirements.

Intrusion detection

• The supplier must specify the name and version of the anti-virus software(s) used.
• The supplier must deploy comprehensive end-point software, preferably in a three-tiered deployment (i.e. at the gateway, server, and client-level), and preferably using industry approved products and information security best practice.
• The supplier must demonstrate the ability to scan all documents for malicious code that are to be posted for download on your behalf.
• The supplier must demonstrate the ability to scan all outgoing messages for malicious code (e.g. e-mails) sent on your behalf.

General Requirements

• The supplier must be compliant with related regulatory requirements (e.g. Payment Card Industry Data Security Standard) if applicable.

• The supplier must provide documentation, similar to a Statement of Work (SOW), detailing the technologies, infrastructure, business arrangement, workflow, schedule, etc.

• If the supplier's contract with your organisation is hosting data classification of highly confidential or sensitive information, the supplier must complete an annual audit by a nationally recognised information security firm to certify compliance with all requirements. The supplier and your organisation must agree upon the selected audit firm prior to the audit.

• The supplier must complete the initial audit within one (1) year of the contract signing date.

• The supplier must agree to the following audit methodology: British Standard (BS) ISO 27001, Code of practice for information security management statement on Accounting Standards (SAS) 70 Type II – if its control objectives match ISO 27001.

The above checklists will provide you with a basic framework regarding the commencement of your supplier assurances processes. However, this is not in any way complete and must be tweaked to cover your specific circumstances and based upon the supplier services you are consuming.

A very important area that you will want to probe with your supplier is how they manage credentials and support the service via multi factor authentication (MFA). We touched on this topic earlier within the cloud API space. MFA is in essence a pre-requisite security control for all access and services outside of your trust boundary. In simple terms, if you are accessing services outside of your organisation via the internet over a VPN or MPLS – MFA is mandatory and may be deployed via a token based approach, or by one of the many applications that can support MFA e.g. by a client certificate that is installed on your device to provide authentication. What is important here is that MFA is available and that the method used to achieve this, whilst it needs to be secure and reviewed, the objective is that when you login to a service you need:

- A Username
- A Password
- A Third piece of information (Third factor) – sometimes a SMS, a voice call asking you to press a number on your phone, a token or fob.

The clear benefit of MFA is that should someone have access to your Username/ and or Password, they cannot access the organisations services or assets, as they will not have the token or fob – the third piece of information. Services within your service provider network will have users access, such as Admin, Support and operator roles.

User access management or UAM is the process of managing access in a secure industry best practice aligned approach.

A lot of suppliers now make extensive use of federated identities and identity access management as a topic in its own right. For now, we need to ensure that user access is set correctly and the principle of Least-Privilege is adopted, which is to limit the user to the absolute level of access he or she requires to perform a job function. In summary, we are looking at a need-to-know basis – we look to provide access on what a user needs to do within their job profile and what they need to know.

It is also quite close to what is known as role based access control or RBAC. To ensure best practice you should audit these processes to ensure effective compliance and look at the details and specifics on how Starters, Leavers and Movers (SLAMs) are managed, both within your on-site systems and the systems that are being managed on your behalf via a service provider. Too often we hear about data breaches whereby a stale account with weak passwords was brute forced and then used to make in-roads to a full data compromise.

It is quite common for organisations to have gaps in this area and some get it right and some don't. They have the correct levels of access but will not revoke or limit the access when a user leaves the organisation or the department. Stale users if not addressed– a term sometimes used to describe this concern increases your attack surface area; therefore, any opportunity to address this area of user access management will without doubt reduce possibility of a data breach.

TAKE HOME

- Verify your supplier's state of securtiy controls that protect your data by requesting attestations of compliance, such as PCI DSS and NIST 800-53 and other relevant standards.

- Perform detailed supplier assurance audits and track any gaps with requests for information, if you are not sure about how your supplier is managing data security.

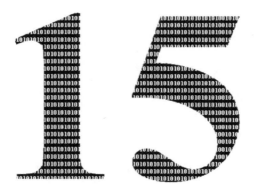

Breach day. Incident Management

So far we have looked at a number of critical areas, security methodologies and advice centred around techniques on reducing your breach susceptibility. We have gone through a number of check lists to help provide a basic understanding of the key processes, such as a procedure for asset management, security testing vulnerability management and patch management etc. As security consultants, these areas are generally themes that should be matured within every organisation, and as they improve general information security is improved and mature practices will start to develop. The end effect of this is that your organisation will be on the way to an overall solid framework that covers its people, processes and technology.

In the spirit of the checklists provided throughout this book, it will be useful to look at the actual process from discovering a data breach and classifying or calling out the breach as a security incident. In other words, when we are notified that the organisation has been compromised and that a data breach has occurred what are the next steps? This whole area is called incident management or incident response. Incident management is a huge topic and hundreds if not thousands of books, articles, journals and courses are available to address this space. Our objective is to look at the data breach from a few angles. Starting with the fundamental question of how will we know when a data breach has occurred?

There are various patterns that will signify that you have been a victim of a data breach, and we use a popular reference for this, which is known as the Indicators of Compromise or (IOC). IOC is a technical term used to define the particular characteristics of the data breach, the signature, the description of what took place, the type of attack, i.e. Physical theft or malware attack via phishing, etc.

Data breaches or notifications of data breaches can come from various entities. We have listed the following to start and provoke your thinking.

In terms of identifying the particular incident we have: -

- Regulatory bodies
- Own Staff
- Customers
- Media
- Law Enforcement
- Hacker teams – extortion.

Working through a few of the above reporting sources let's take a look at the regulatory bodies. If you are processing credit card information you will be required to comply with the payment card industry data security standard. PCI-DSS as we discussed earlier is designed to reduce payment fraud and support card data protection. If customers experience credit card fraud they will call their bank to explain that their card has been used fraudulently. The bank will in turn call the payment service provider, acquirer or issuer. These are card payment terms, although in essence credit cards are issued by a bank but authorised by Visa, Master Card and other payment schemes.

The point is that the banks that issue cards are governed by regulatory bodies that investigate fraud. When fraud is detected, they will carry out their own independent research in some cases and decide whether a data breach has occurred or not. They will then notify your organisation.

In many cases where organisations have effective monitoring operations, they have powerful data mining and analytics tools looking at Firewalls, Intrusion systems and Malware detection being monitored 24/7/365. Sometimes called security operations centres (SOCs), if you are lucky enough to have a SOC, the SOC will look for Indicators of Compromise (IOCs) across your network for technical attacks that you may yourself discover. Rich dashboards are presented showing live network activity and malware incidents, which are investigated on an incident basis. Therefore, data breaches can be reported by a number of channels. Increasingly, we are also seeing in the wild malicious threat actors, such as hackers simply sending the management an e-mail saying they have their records and sometimes attempt extortion with your data. On occasions, they will actually release a sample into the public domain to force you to comply with their requests. How to deal with this scenario and the pros and cons needs a full detailed response but the clear message is to not engage with any malicious hacker group without involvement of law enforcement, who have dedicated teams to deal with these sorts of requests.

Many organisations have incident reporting, incident response teams (IRTs) and other supporting security incident reporting functions. Some aspects of incident reporting are hugely complex; therefore it is fair to say from experience that some company plans have thirty-page incident plans, which can sometimes detract from the basic requirement of how we deal with an incident.

An incident management framework should be created and followed by all (employees, contractors or 3rd parties) performing work for and handling information on behalf of the organisation and/or its affiliates or service providers. (Incident response should be a corner stone of your supplier assurance process when validating the security of external providers, including cloud service providers).

An incident is defined as an occurrence that actually or potentially:

- Jeopardises personal safety
- Violates personal privacy
- Impacts on the confidentiality, integrity or availability of information – Technical attacks
- Violates policies, procedures and/or standards
- Breaches the terms of a contract
- Violates any law and/or regulation (local, State, Federal, Provincial, etc.)

A typical incidents workflow diagram is shown below:

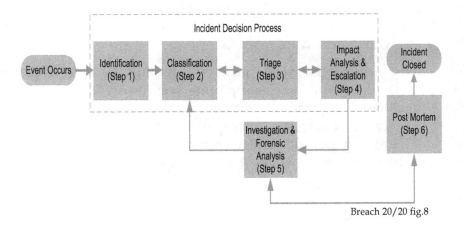

Breach 20/20 fig.8

Incident Decision Process

The incident decision process illustrated provides initial guidance to properly classify, triage and escalate an incident.

This process facilitates response activities across the various departments and business units within your organisation.

A breakdown of the various phases is listed below.

Identification Phase

The following occurs with the *Identification Phase:*

1. An event has occurred.
2. An individual has observed the event.
3. An individual believes the event is an incident and warrants investigation.
4. The individual reports the event to your organisation or department.
5. The incident response process is initiated.

Classification Phase

As part of the classification process each incident should be classified into "Categories" and "Asset Types" defined as follows:

> ➢ Theft/Loss
>> • Hardware – physical equipment (e.g. laptop, phone, backup, removal media, such as USB sticks) has been lost or stolen.

- Piracy – Software that is copyrighted or patented has been stolen, or a violation of an End-User Licence Agreement (EULA) has occurred. Keys and licence numbers for applications or commercial off the shelf software (COTS) has been stolen.

➤ Unauthorised Access
  - Electronic – The confidentiality of information has been or potentially will be compromised, as a result of user(s) having unauthorised access to a system and/or data.
  - Physical Environment – An unauthorised person has gained access to a restricted or controlled area.

➤ Service Disruption
  - Electronic – A service or application has failed, is unavailable, or has degraded to an unacceptable level of operation as a result of equipment failure, network outage, system or application error, excessive usage, or as a consequence of a distributed denial of service attack.

➤ Policy Violation – A worker has violated an organisational policy. For example, a staff member has used a personal USB device on a corporate laptop and copied company data to the USB device.

➤ Personal Safety
  - Employee – A worker's personal safety has been jeopardised due to a physical threat.

➤ Privacy – Private information of an individual used within the organisation, including staff details has been, or has the potential to be used/ exposed to others.

  - Personal Identifiable Information (PII) – Information that can be used to uniquely identify, contact or locate a single person, or can be used with other sources to uniquely identify a single individual e.g. name, driver's licence number, date of birth, credit card numbers, digital identity, fingerprints, National Insurance numbers, passport details and other forms of identification.

- Payment Card Industry (PCI) – Card holder data, including Primary Account Number (PAN), Card holder Name, Expiration Date, CVC,CVC2 numbers, PIN etc.

➤ Data Breach– system or systems and/or its data has been compromised – Any type of compromise, whether a technical attack or other, for example data loss through loosing media etc. is included.

- Public – The system or data is classified as "PUBLIC".
- Company Confidential – The system or data is classified as "CONFIDENTIAL" and contains organisational company records or the organisation's Intellectual Property (IP).
- Client Confidential - Any data contained on organisation's system is considered sensitive to the customer.

Triage Phase

Once the incident has been classified, it will be triaged to the appropriate internal departments and/or business units (BU) or departments. Incidents reported by external entities or law enforcement are reported directly to the CEO, Legal department and the Chief Security Information Officer (CISO)

Impact Analysis and Escalation Phase

Impact Analysis

As a rule of thumb incidents should be analysed to determine the impact to the business to ensure appropriate escalation to senior management and legal personnel. A simple matrix that you have derived from your asset management and data classification activities may help you list out what criticality and the severity of the risk an incident is based on. In other words, what is the perceived impact on the organisation, its assets, and the criticality of the asset?

To further clarify this area, which is often overlooked – we have lost data – in order to determine how important that data was we look at the classification. Were the data credit cards? Were the data HR staff records? Or, were they Usernames and Passwords for your customers for the software as a service (SaaS) your paying customers use and buy from you?

Once we know what was lost and how important that data was we can start to decide on the impact, the communications back to the client, if required, informing regulatory bodies and in some case law enforcement.

Incident Escalation and Management Team

The risk rating used as a basis to determine the proper escalation of the incident is as follows, and can be adjusted as required. Obviously not all the listed roles will apply to your organisation.

- Level 0-1: The incident will be handled by the IT Service Desk or the customer service and support lines.
- Level 2: The incident will be handled by the department or business unit Incident Coordinator (IC).
- Level 3: The incident will be escalated by the IC to a Sr. Manager of the department or business unit.
- Level 4: The incident will be escalated to a VP of the department or business unit.
- Level 5: The incident will be escalated to a senior and executive department or business unit members.

The individuals formulated during this process are considered the Incident Management Team (IMT) and have the following roles and responsibilities:

- IT Service Desk: generally, *handles level 0-1 risks through standard operational procedures. (Some organisations actually outsource level 1 and 2 and other incidents to a third party either with an on-site presence or remotely via a help desk number. Those staff generally have VPN links to the enterprise and can assist staff who escalate incidents to them.*

- Incident Coordinator (IC): It is the incident co-coordinators job to co-ordinate all aspects of the incident management process from discovery to resolutions.

  - Serves as the first line of communication
  - Updating the Incident Response Report
  - Allocating a risk rating to the incident
  - Escalating the incident according to the risk rating
  - Updating members of the IMT
  - Triaging the incident to other departments and business units if required

In many organisations the Chief Information Security Officer (CISO) coordinates the security function.

The CISO will generally participate in the following incident management activities:

- Providing direction to the Senior Managers
- Assessing and providing the final determination of the risk to the company
- Directly communicating incident status with VP/SVPs and Executive Management
- Participating in communications plans in coordination with Legal team and senior executive management
- Communicating with outside third parties and law enforcement
- Addressing privacy incidents with Legal Teams
- Co-ordinating follow-up forensics investigations

Post-Mortem Phase

All incidents require a post-mortem exercise prior to incident closure. Post incident analysis is a crucial aspect of incident management.

Learning from failures via an open loop forum with all key participants is a unique learning experience that will help you dissect the particular incident and use the rich data to modify and adjust your security models. This will also allow the organisation to evolve with a constant improvement across your people, processes and technology.

Failure learning is key in many industries – if we take a look at the airline industry (who openly and activity embrace failure management), we can see great improvements and detailed learning from every air traffic incident, crash, near miss or other failures, as an open book. Most incidents within the airline industry are almost immediately written up and shared, in some cases within hours, for every pilot to look at instantly.

The benefit from this open book approach goes against the grain of blame management. Obviously, if there are lessons that need to be learned where processes were not followed, then people may be disciplined as a deterrent.

Conversely, if we look at other industries we still see opportunities for huge improvement in failure learning. For example, the health sector loses patients every day across the world, as a result of medical negligence, failure to follow procedures that result in catastrophic outcomes and in many cases fatalities.

Obviously the industries cited as an example of failure learning have at the centre stage critical activities i.e. activities that directly relate to mortality rates. If a pilot makes a mistake there will more than likely be fatalities as there will be in the health sector.

Loosing data or experiencing a data breach does not result in fatalities in general terms, but that does not mean organisations ignore and do not implement failure learning procedures.

Mock-Intrusion Testing Phase

As a result of the previous incident response sample framework our objective is to establish standardised essential practices with regard to Incident Response and then communicate awareness of those requirements throughout the organisation.

In order to fully initialise a best-of-breed Incident Response program and reach a ready-for-service state, it is important to regularly test the level of adherence to the IR Planning policies that have been created.

In my experience I have found that perhaps the most effective, not to mention cheapest, method of testing for policy compliance in the areas of Incident Response, is to conduct a mock-hack or intrusion.

When conducted in coordination with IT management, the mock-hack can be an effective tool for measuring the level of response to an incident, as well as the Customer Incident Response Team's familiarity with documented response procedures.

The objective is to ensure the intrusion attempt is well coordinated and is carried out by Internal teams from the organisation.

Methodology

Pre-arranging a mock-hack or security-related incident in coordination with IT management allows your organisation's Investigative Response personnel to co-ordinate the corresponding response elements.

This allows IT management the ability to monitor the level of response that ensues, as well as the level of adherence to your policies and procedures.

The teams involved should then provide management with constructive criticism and remarks intended to better set your IR program for success in responding to real future security incidents.

A simple checklist to support the mock testing is shown below.

Team Responsibilities:

The IRT agrees to:

1.   Be responsible for and facilitate all communications across involved management personnel;

2.   Make a best effort to ensure that IT technical personnel are not aware of the testing exercise.

3.   Provide relevant access to protected data centre areas and Customer Incident Response team personnel during the mock-intrusion. (Note any access created must be documented and removed immediately after the mock testing. – remember what SLAMs are?)

4.   Be responsible for the decision to implement (or not to implement) recommendations, the actions taken to do so, and the results achieved from such implementation. Failure learning!

- Clearly define roles and incident triage but keep it as simple as possible to deal with a data breach.

- Have a documented approach to dealing with customer data breach announcements, with approval from your CEO, HR and legal teams.

- Do not communicate with hackers under any circumstance, even if they claim they will help you secure your systems and/ or work for an organisation that specialises in security. If they have hacked your site then they may have committed a criminal offence.

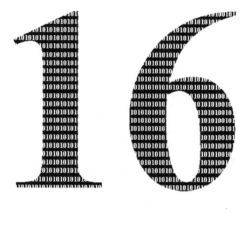

Checkpoint

In the previous chapters, we looked at a target approach on how we may respond to an incident. There are many potential frameworks for incident response and we must look to create an incident response approach based upon the size, culture and hierarchy of the organisation. The take home however, is that by adopting an approach to dealing with incidents and then following up with post incident analysis i.e. what went wrong? How did it happen? And, what evidence has been collected? i.e. The indicators of compromise recommended are absolutely key. As suggested, the mock testing approach is also extremely useful and a technique I use to this day when consulting. Simply put – let's say we have an incident at 2.45 pm today. What do we do?

You will learn a great deal from the mock testing, both positive and negative – the key however is to be constructive and positive, as well as progressive. How you deal with the incident in mock testing will equate to how you deal with the incident in real terms should a data breach or related incident occur.

We are now on the cusp of actually seeing how well our organisation is dealing with information security – we spoke about maturity of controls and we looked at how we should aim at least to have repeatable defined processes and supported high level policy statements.

So let's start to look at this in more depth.

Our next objective is to determine the state of information security within our organisation relative to best security practices. This analysis may also examine the security organisation, its reporting structure, and the available resources dedicated to the protection of the company's information assets.

The assessment approach, covering the ten categories of security controls listed below will be considered and an overall control rating determined. The analysis of the control ratings can also result in individual risks being identified and rated as High, Medium or Low. Each type of security control assessed should be rated as one of:

- No evidence found;
- Minimal controls in place;
- Fair controls in place;
- Sound controls in place; and
- Best practice.

The table below is taken directly from ISO 27001 – Information security standard. The ISO 27000 family of standards helps organisations keep information assets secure.

Control Category	
Security Policy	Organisational Security
Asset Classification and Control	Physical and Environmental Security
Personnel Security	Access Control
Communications and Operations Management	System Development and Maintenance
Compliance	Business Continuity Management

Using this family of standards will help your organisation manage its security of assets, such as financial information, intellectual property, employee details or information entrusted to you by third parties. ISO/IEC 27001 is the best-known standard in the family providing requirements for an information security management system (ISMS).

A deep dive into the standard is outside of the scope of this book and under each category listed below there are some 220 plus controls, which are available from various sources on the internet, such as the British Standards Institute (BSI).

A great deal of organisations actually hire ISO 27001 auditors to perform an assessment of the categories below and he or she is certified in the audit of ISO 27001. To start though you can perform a basic assessment yourself. This is the tip of the ice-berg, but to get things going remember we are looking at each category and simply asking ourselves in each category where do we feel the organisation is? We can use the following labels to decide on what we can observe.

• No evidence found;
• Minimal controls in place;
• Fair controls in place;
• Sound controls in place; and
• Best practice. List same as before?

I have added some details to each category to bring various elements of the book we have already covered into play.

It may be that you will have varying degrees of compliance with each area and it is fine to list them out. For example, you may say fair controls in place for vulnerability management and minimal controls in place for patching. Feel free to add a few more columns to the right to collect more information. The key here is that you are assessing your information security to get a feel of what maturity you have. What we are doing is bringing together capability maturity in a simple way, which is quite novel and I have endeavoured to explain key concepts in the most basic and clear terms by encouraging you to think of assessing your security. If you download the official ISO 27001 standard you will be able to obtain a list of all controls which can be audited. The ISO 27001 auditor job however is the job of a trained, skilled resource. Certainly an area you can move into and very interesting work by the way.

Additionally, we can expand a little to help guide the assessment by listing out some of the areas included under each heading:

- **Security Policy**

    o High level policy statement

    o Policy hierarchy

    o Organisation of Information Security

    o Roles and responsibilities

    o Confidentiality agreements

    o External links to suppliers

    o Reviews and Risk Assessments

    o External Parties

- **Asset Management**

  - Inventory of Assets

  - Ownership and Custodianship

  - Information Classification

- **Human Resources Security**

  - Pre-Employment

  - During employment

  - Post-employment

- **Physical and Environmental Security**

  - Secure Areas

  - Equipment Security

- **Communications and Operations Security**

  - General Principles (i.e. operating procedures, split between test and prod, segregation of duties)

  - Change Management

  - System Acceptance

  - Third Party Service Delivery

  - Capacity Planning

  - Protection against malicious code / mobile code (i.e. Anti-virus)

- o Information Back-up

- o Network Security

- o Media Handling

- o Exchange of Information

- o Electronic Trading

- o System Monitoring (i.e. logs, audit trails and their protection)

- o Access Control

- o Access Control Policy

- o User Access Management

- o User Responsibilities (including password guidelines)

- o Network Access Control

- o Operating System Access Control

- o Application and Information Access Control

- o Mobile Computing and Teleworking

- o Information Systems Acquisition, Development and Maintenance

- o System Requirements of Information Systems

- o Application Controls

- o Cryptographic Controls

o   Security of System Files

o   Security in Development and Support Processes

o   Information Security Incident Management

o   Reporting Security Events and Weaknesses

o   Management of Information Security Incidents and Improvements

o   Business Continuity Management

o   Information Security Aspects of BCM

o   Compliance

o   Compliance with Legal Requirements

o   Compliance with Security Policies and Standards, and Technical Compliance

o   Information Systems Audit Considerations

The above list can actually be expanded further into granular and ISO 27001 controls as stated but at least we now have much more detail to work with to carry out your assessment.

Question – do security frameworks, such as the ISO 27001 help reduce your data breach attack surface area?

Yes, they do as you have a formal stated information security model that is incrementally improved, which will reduce your attack surface area.

That does not however mean that organisations that are ISO 27001 compliant or compliant with the myriad of other compliance mandates are not going to experience a data breach – in fact many of the larger organisations at the sharp end of large data breaches had a tick in the box for a great number of standards and attestations including (but not limited to) the ISO 27001 standard.

You can be forgiven if you are now thinking how come these organisations were hacked and ended up with a data breach, if they had robust and measured security controls?

The answer lies in the parallel worlds of attack patterns and compliance standards, such as the ISO 27001. The ISO 27001 is essentially a governance standard and whilst compliance will provide a view of your holistic security processes – generally speaking if you have a ISO 27001 compliant framework in your organisation you are doing well and this is part of your governance. Having security frameworks based upon ISO 27001 will support your efforts and work towards data breach reduction strategies. In the industry what we see mostly is organisations that have fragmented security programmes i.e. organisations that have implemented security practices in some, but not all areas, are the ones that experience data breaches.

However, given the sophistications of the attacks and the techniques used by malwares, Trojans and exploit kits moving data around your network ready for offloading, to beat these approaches we need regular deep security testing. This testing, as we covered in the security testing chapters, needs to look at the cyber security kill chain in detail. Test scripts, tools and techniques should be used that simulates attack patterns across the kill chain. Couple this with vulnerability management and we are now moving to solid layered security defences. The ISO 27001 standard is the glue that brings together the end-to-end security processes across your organisation.

By converging the governance standards with detailed security testing we are operating a secure operating environment. This is by and large the reason why organisations that have compliant security frameworks and security management systems still experience a data breach. They pay lip service to the standard get a tick in the box – do the minimum but continue to have porous untested network defences within internal and external defences. To be fair, we also have a great deal of organisations that get the mix right – they have robust governance frameworks and detailed technical test strategies that are automated with active alerting and monitoring.

We mentioned security operations centres or SOCs before – these will only exist in organisations that have very high value data and significant security investment, such as global banks and other very high profile organisations , for instance huge retailers. These tier 1 organisations mostly get it right because they have; the critical thinking, they know the value of their data, they have the best staff, they have huge security budgets, they have strategic as well as tactical approaches and they regularly test their security internally and externally. They have a great deal to lose if they are breached and their data ends up with the bad guys or on the internet.

Remember we stated earlier "The cost of protection vs. the Cost of Loss". If the value of our data is very high, we are going to do everything in our capability and capacity to protect it.

Small to medium enterprises and other small organisations won't have the huge spend or best staff – so what is the thinking to support these organisations? Well remember again we said the most data compromises, in fact 96 % occurred through lack of simple controls.

Get the basics right and you're in a good place. Teach your teams about risks, threats and vulnerabilities and update your security defences. Standing still in information security is actually going backwards, because the risks are changing every day and threats are evolving – your security must react and evolve to match these changes. Change is the only certainty (within the hacking context). Your security controls must change and evolve based upon new risks.

A distributed denial of service attack (DDoS) previously may have made extensive use of amplifications attacks using protocols, such as DNS and SNMP. A very recent attack, which took place was over 600 plus Gbps– that's over half a terabyte of traffic being sent to a single IP or a number of IPs. What did this huge DDoS attack use for this amount of illegal traffic being pointed towards the victim? It used online devices connected to the internet, such as cameras and other Internet of Things (IoTs) devices.

The tools and approaches that are utilised to execute the attacks are easily available to anyone and offer anonymity and the potential to easily break the internet, or at least your online presence, if it is not suitably protected.

The table that follows lists the categories where your assessments should be added.

Control Category Control Rating	Control Assessment
Security Policy – Do you have one? Do you update it ?	?
Organisational Security – Policies, processes and procedures to support information security	?
Asset Classification and control	?
Personnel Security	?
Physical and Environmental Security – Escorts for data centres and security as well as visitor badges ?	?

Communications and Operations Management - Patch management, Vulnerability management ? do you scan for vulnerabilities ?	?
Access Control	?
System Development and Maintenance - Source code testing	?
Business Continuity Management	?
Compliance - Any regulatory compliances, such as PCI DSS	?

Completed high level assessment with sample control ratings.

Control Category	Control Rating
Security Policy	Minimal security controls in place
Organisational Security	Fair security controls in place
Asset Classification and Control	Minimal security controls in place
Personnel Security	Fair security controls in place
Physical and Environmental Security	Fair security controls in place
Communications and operations management	Fair security controls in place
Access control	Fair security controls in place
System Development and maintenance	Fair security controls in place
Business Continuity Management	Minimal security controls in place
Compliance	Sound security controls in place

The above completed high level assessment shows the relevant domains against the control ratings. This assessment may be used as an organisational check list to help you see where your security is good and needs to be maintained, or not so good and in need of urgent improvement.

I started to write this book with the single objective of providing an easy to read breakdown of important topics that you need to address to improve your information security. Keeping it light touch where possible, I have provided many checklists, which you can tweak and adapt as required. At a minimum, it will provoke your thought into more research, which will hopefully lead to an increase in your understanding and knowledge of a the particular chapter.

There are hundreds of books that cover cyber security, networking and active defence that you may look to for additional insight. This book is the tip of the iceberg. It has incorporated a style of writing and use of examples and relevant charts etc. to make it as easy as possible for the reader to learn the basic approach to information security and use that information to help reduce the possibility of data breaches. Furthermore, I consciously stayed at a level to both appeal to security centric thinkers i.e. consultants, but also none security staff, such as senior managers, and IT teams.

I have greatly enjoyed the experience of writing this book and sincerely hope that it adds value to you and your organisation at some level.

By educating your workforce on the risks of how a simple mistake or hacking attempt can lead to a data breach is critical.

Security awareness and regular staff campaigns informing your staff on how the organisation deals with sensitive information, and what the organisation policies are, should be ingrained in your team, staff induction and hiring processes.

There is no panacea for data breach prevention. Data breach prevention is a number of critical parts working together many of which are listed in this book. Information Security is not just the responsibility of your security team or the chief security officer – It is **everybody's** responsibility.

NOTES

Feel free to use these pages to jot down notes or scribble to your heart's content…

NOTES

NOTES

NOTES

NOTES

NOTES

NOTES

NOTES

NOTES

NOTES

NOTES

Index

www.ingramcontent.com/pod-product-compliance
Lightning Source LLC
LaVergne TN
LVHW022306060326
832902LV00020B/3294